THE ART OF CHINESE COOKING

The Art of

CHINESE

COOKING

by Mimie Ouei

illustrated by Jeanyee Wong

RANDOM HOUSE

Fourth Printing

© Copyright, 1960, by Mimie Ouei

All rights reserved under International and Pan-American Copyright
Conventions. Published in New York by Random House, Inc., and
simultaneously in Toronto, Canada, by Random House of Canada,
Limited.

Library of Congress Catalog Card Number: 60-5561

Portions of this book were published originally in *Woman's Day*.

Manufactured in the United States of America by
The Colonial Press Inc.

My thanks are due to the many friends who through the years have generously furnished me with their recipes, and especially to my father who, after threescore years and ten of cooking by feel, painstakingly measured each ingredient and set it down on paper for my benefit. My grateful acknowledgments are also due to the many for their suggestions and assistance and especially, in this connection, to Frank Latham.

To my cousin, Huang Dan-tsae, I make my kowtows for the best calligraphy outside of mainland China.

TO MY MOTHER WHO ENCOURAGED ME
AND MY FATHER WHO TAUGHT ME ✳

FOREWORD

The delights of our native cuisine are no longer readily available
to those of us Chinese who are forced to live abroad. If we want
to savor genuine Chinese home cooking, we have to prepare it
ourselves. Most of the Chinese who crossed the ocean to the
United States for higher education, and those who came later as
political refugees, had never cooked before. In fact, they had no
familiarity with the kitchen. My mother was sixty before she
learned to cook, and then only as a challenge. She wanted to
show us she could change with changing times, and to prove that
anything can be done if you set your mind to it.

The servants' quarters and the kitchen were a realm unknown
to all members of the family. No one intruded into these private
quarters and definitely not into the cook's empire. In a typical
Chinese house, the kitchen was many courtyards away. It might
even be in another building. Or, if the compound was not that
big, then the kitchen was at least many corridors away.

Every well-to-do home had a *Ta Shih Fu* or chief cook and
at least two assistants who helped with such tasks as washing and

cutting the vegetables, slicing the meat and preparing the other ingredients. The *Ta Shih Fu* would do the marketing, deposit his purchases in the kitchen and tell his assistants what to do, then disappear until it was time for the actual cooking. Gradually, he would leave more and more to the assistants, till they could take over full responsibility. In their apprenticeship to the chef, the assistants would slowly pick up tricks of the trade. Thus the techniques of cooking were passed from one generation of cooks to another, and for this reason have thrived for thousands of years without the benefit of any cookbook.

Luckily for me, my family lived abroad for many years, and the chef and the kitchen were much closer at hand. Otherwise, I would not have known very much about the practical side of the Chinese cuisine, for I would have been subject to the same customs that prevailed for other girls of my age.

My father was in the diplomatic service and so we lived abroad, where it was quite *comme il faut* for the daughter of the house to be in and out of the kitchen at any time. My father has served his country for forty years in every continent but one. He has dined with kings, emperors and czars; he has known the best of all cuisines and has been one of the real gourmets of his time. Every cook he instructed, whether Chinese, Italian, French or Austrian, went away having gained something by this contact. But our very own chef who traveled with us all over the world was Ah Hing. He was a good friend as well as a marvelous *Ta Shih Fu*. He accepted my frequent invasions of the kitchen with incomparable patience (which I took for granted until I met a French chef who was not above throwing knives at intruders). From Ah Hing I learned the art of cooking, even as I learned the value of good food from my father.

So while my memory is still clear, and before Ah Hing's techniques and subtle flavors are forgotten, I hasten to record a few observations from a happier day, lest the benefits of our association be altogether lost.

Mimie Ouei

New York, N.Y.
April, 1960

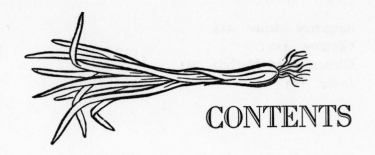

CONTENTS

PART THREE ✱

PART * I

YIN, AN
INTRODUCTION

Pleasure in food has been part of the Chinese culture for centuries. We respect food in the way we respect learning and knowledge, and it takes a prominent place as a subject for conversation. From the lowliest peasant to the red-buttoned mandarin, the Chinese have always been gourmets. It was not unusual for us to see a farmer bringing a chicken or a fisherman his catch to a restaurant and instructing the cook how he would like it prepared. This same man might live in a hovel and have no other clothes than those he was wearing, but he knew how his food should be cooked and served.

The Chinese think that since one must eat to live, one may as well eat well if he can. And to eat well, one must know the fundamentals of cooking. The Chinese, even those who do not cook, seem instinctively to understand the art of cooking. It was quite fascinating for me to listen to one of my aunts giving detailed instructions to her chef regarding the preparation of certain

3

dishes. He was a Chinese equivalent of a *cordon bleu,* and generations of chefs had graduated from his kitchen, yet he used to nod in agreement with certain of her suggestions to improve a dish. And the amazing part of it all was that she had never entered a kitchen. Later, I found that many such women knew the art of cooking theoretically, although they were never called upon to perform it practically.

There were no recorded recipes of the Chinese cuisine until the twentieth century, and even then only in Western countries. In China, cooking was done by feel and taste, and its secrets were passed on from one generation to another. Having tasted the same dishes made from the same recipes, we have come to the conclusion that cooking *à la Chinoise* is not an exact science and that a dish cannot be reproduced like a chemical formula. The ingredients, the cooking time and the amount of heat will vary under different conditions.

The Chinese cuisine has been compared with the French. The food of both countries is characterized by unique flavors and a simplicity that belies the work involved in the preparation. Simplicity to a Chinese cook does not mean opening a can or defrosting a package of frozen vegetables. It is achieved by much patience and care. Chinese chefs, like French chefs, believe that good cooking consists of making the best use of the ingredients at hand. Therefore, they know that the preparation begins before the kitchen is reached, and that the selection of ingredients is most important. It is the practice of Chinese cooks to adapt the method of cooking to the ingredients and not the ingredients to the method. They believe that the cooking should enhance the natural taste of the raw materials. Taste is what gives us enjoyment, and it is up to the cook to give food that taste. The ultimate test of a good Chinese cook is whether he can make something out of an egg and some broth. If he can create something wonderful out of two such simple things, then he is indeed a cook.

The differences between Chinese and Western cooking are many, but among the most noticeable are these: In Western cooking, the meat and vegetables are not cut up into bite-sized pieces. They come to the table whole and are cut at the table. Pepper and salt are usually added at table. In Chinese cooking, the bite-sized pieces of meat and vegetables are seasoned while cooking. The advantage of the small pieces is that the meat and vegetables can be cooked in a short time, thus retaining their juices, tenderness and nutrients. The seasoning added during cooking permeates each piece of meat and vegetable and makes the flavor more appetizing and the aroma more stimulating.

Since it is the method of cooking that is basic, rather than the material or ingredients used, nine out of ten of the dishes in this book can be cooked with foodstuffs we use in America every day, and most of the ingredients in the recipes are available any time of the year. Chinese cooking, besides being attractive, is practicable and is no mystery of the Orient. It is not made up of putting a lot of exotic things together like wood ear and lotus seeds, but is more a matter of cooking technique.

Another difference between the Chinese and Western modes of cooking is that in Chinese dishes the meat and vegetables are cooked together, thus allowing a small amount of meat to go a long way. Meat and vegetables lend each other flavor. In Western cooking, with a few exceptions such as certain kinds of stews and the French *pot-au-feu*, the meat and vegetables are cooked separately but eaten together.

The Chinese season their food during cooking because they believe that the heat produces a chemical reaction on the condiment which will enhance the natural taste of the food and get rid of unpleasant odors. The secret of taste depends on the mastery of combining certain foods with certain seasonings without the condiment betraying itself. Once you have mastered this technique, you can, with a little ingenuity, concoct hundreds of variations from one basic recipe. The Chinese are ingenious experimenters, and as China is a poor country, the necessity for economizing, experimenting and innovating has caused the Chinese to develop an unsurpassed and varied cuisine.

The Chinese feel that no gathering is complete without a meal. They like to show off their chef as they would a favorite child, and a chef is considered good when he can prepare a meal at short notice; can prepare an appetizing dish; can make a dish out of everyday material at a minimum cost.

It has often been said that the Chinese, men and women alike, look younger than their years. We attribute this to our food. Although we may not talk about food in a scientific way, we have arrived at a well-balanced diet. It is almost impossible to find an unbalanced Chinese dinner, what with the mode of cooking and variety of dishes. Today this is recognized by nutritionists.

It is interesting to note that in the last twenty years there has been a rapid expansion of interest in Chinese food, not only in the United States but over the whole world. You will find, in most major cities, at least one fashionable restaurant which is Chinese. This interest is amazing when you think that there has been no organized promotional movement to popularize the Chinese cuisine. Let us see then how the cuisine grew and prospered in the United States.

It is said that the first Chinese was brought to the United States by one of Vincent Astor's sailing ships. He was willing to come because, besides being venturesome, he hailed from the district of Toyshan near Canton and the Cantonese have always been seafaring people. Toyshan had never been very productive so its people were forced to seek their fortunes elsewhere. This immigrant was the first of thousands to come to this country. They reached the Golden Gate early in the 1800s and came as prospectors of gold and as laborers on the first transcontinental railroad. Others became market gardeners and worked on the huge farms of California. As one member of the family made good, he sent back for a brother or a cousin, and this migration became a steady flow till the harsh Exclusion Act of 1882.

The United States authorities, having encouraged immigration and having brought in cheap labor, wanted to keep these people happy. So Chinese cooks were brought to the United States.

They opened up independent restaurants on the roads and in the gold fields. This was then the first phase of the introduction of Chinese cuisine into this country. The food was prepared for Chinese customers who demanded food as prepared in their villages near Canton.

Into one of these little shacks in the gold fields came three Americans one evening, demanding food. It was after hours and the kitchen was closed. The men, however, were very hungry and tipsy and would not be put off. Restaurants were few and far between, and if they didn't get food at this particular place, they would have to go without food all night. They refused to leave, so the cook in desperation went into the kitchen to see what he had. There was nothing to serve except the remains of a few dishes. He threw them all together, brought the mixture out piping hot, and served it with rice. The three men threw themselves on this dish greedily and enjoyed it so much that they asked for its name so that they could order it again. On the spur of the moment, the cook said, "Chop suey," which in Cantonese means odds and ends; and there a new dish was born. The fame of this dish and others concocted for the American taste spread far and wide, and this type of cooking still remains with us, as testified by the small chop suey houses throughout the country.

The next phase developed at the end of World War II. Men who had seen service in the China-Burma-India theater were not satisfied with the chow mien, egg rolls and fried rice which the Chinese restaurants had been serving them. They started to demand, describe and order dishes which they had tasted in China, and the restaurant owners were quick to understand that they had to contend with a new type of customer. The Americans had come of age in the Chinese cuisine and had become gourmets.

And it is only a short step from dining authentically in a Chinese restaurant to wanting to prepare these dishes yourself. The fad of do-it-yourself has reached Chinese cuisine, and the housewife, bachelor and career girl alike have taken up the challenge. Hence this cookbook!

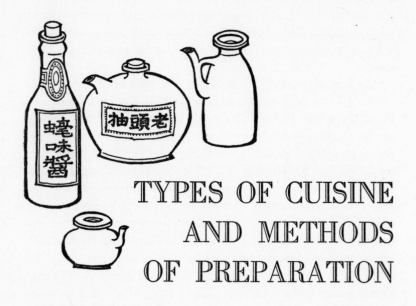

TYPES OF CUISINE
AND METHODS
OF PREPARATION

Until recently, most of the Chinese the Americans came into contact with were Cantonese. Thus the Americans would not have been far wrong if they thought that all Chinese looked alike, for these all came from the same district in China. But as Chinese students from other provinces came to the United States and were unable to return to their homeland, and as political refugees arrived, Americans have had to revise their thinking. They have found the Chinese very dissimilar in their physical features and their habits.

Communication in China had always been difficult, so much so that many regions became isolated. The people in these areas adopted different habits and developed a cuisine which adapted itself to the climate and natural resources, as well as to the needs of its people. In general, there were five distinct types of cuisine developed through the centuries, namely, those of Canton, Fukien, Shantung, Honan and Szechuan.

8

Adherents of other types of cooking will be up in arms because their part of the country is not represented, but the fact that a certain region is famous for one or two dishes does not entitle it to the distinction of being designated as a school.

✶ The Cantonese School

The Cantonese school of cooking is the best known outside of China, for the Cantonese were the travelers and the emigrants. This is true as far as the United States, Australia, England and France are concerned.

Canton became rich after her doors were opened to foreign trade. With wealth came leisure and the desire for good food, and through the indulgence of this desire, a cuisine characterized by sautéeing, roasting and grilling was developed. Fried rice and fried noodles are also the specialties of this school.

✶ The Fukien School

We from Fukien think that we have the best cuisine in China. There are not many examples of this type of cooking in the United States, because the Fukienese, who were the sailors of China, settled in Thailand, Malaya and other parts of southeast Asia. This cuisine is characterized by good all-around cooking, although many complain that too many soupy dishes are included in its repertoire. Our cooking also abounds in sea food, since we have a long coastline. Suckling pig and spring rolls are two other well-known dishes from this region. A red fermented bean sauce was a specialty of Foochow and the best soy sauce used to be produced in this part of the country.

✶ The Shantung School

Shantung, besides having produced philosophers, has also produced good cooking. As Peking is so near, many people from Shantung migrated to the big city and took their cooking with them. So although the dishes may have been perfected in Peking, they are native to Shantung. The food in this northern part of the country is lighter than that of the south. Much of it is cooked in wine sauce, and very little sautéeing is done. The most famous dish of all from this region is Peking Duck.

✳ The Honan School

The capital of Honan was once the capital of China, and with the wealthier people flocking to the court, good cooking was in demand. Honan is the home of the sweet-and-sour dishes and the carp from the Yellow River is famous. Kidney sautéed in the sweet-sour manner is a good example of this school.

✳ The Szechuan School

Till Chungking became a temporary capital, Szechuan, in the far west, had been left to her own devices. Its summers are terribly hot and the Szechuanese, like all people who live in hot climates, developed a hot, very highly seasoned cuisine. This is the main characteristic of this school of cooking. Chicken with hot peppers is a good example. Soil in this province is very rich and fungi grow in abundance here.

There are five main methods of preparing food in the Chinese manner, and they are common to all the five schools. They are sautéeing, red cooking (a kind of braising or stewing with soy sauce, known as *hung shao* in Chinese), deep frying, steaming and roasting, barbecuing or grilling. There are many other variations of cooking, of course, but these five main methods cover the field fairly adequately.

✳ Sautéeing

Of the five, the most characteristic method is sautéeing. It is the most difficult of all ways, but its mastery is worth while for it is most versatile. You must learn to judge the degree of fire, the method of cutting the ingredient and its proper thickness, and the order of putting the ingredients into the cooking vessel. These three principles help you to acquire the proper color, flavor and aroma.

The method of sautéeing may again be subdivided: first, into one in which white meat is cooked with salt, and second, one in which dark meat is browned with soy sauce. Tenderness is all-important in this mode of cooking. With meat, use lean filet. Be sure that the meat is cut across the grain into the size desired. It is easier to cut the meat fine when it is slightly frozen. If the meat comes from a deep-freeze, give it time to thaw. If the meat is not as thin as you would like it, pound it with the cleaver. Mix the slices with cornstarch in a little water and soy sauce or oyster sauce. Marinating the meat in the sauce protects the surface of the pieces and keeps in the juice while cooking.

If chicken is your choice, use the breast without the skin. Soak the slices in cold water with a little salt. This will harden the meat and prevent sticking while cooking. Do not use soy sauce with white meat as that would darken the slices.

It is essential that everything be prepared before you start cooking, because ingredients are put in seconds apart, and you do not have time to slice and cut, say, your ginger or bamboo shoots, when you need them. Sliced vegetables, meat and other ingredients should be set out on separate plates and within easy reach.

The straight cutting method is most suitable for tender vegetables—for example, scallions. For harder vegetables, the diagonal method of slicing is better. A larger area cut across the grain will be exposed to the heat and for the absorption of the seasoning and juices. This method of cutting is known as the rolling cut and is suitable for vegetables like carrots and those with long stalks, such as asparagus and broccoli. Use the vegetable chopper and cut off half an inch of the asparagus at an angle, then roll the stalk halfway over and cut again, and so on. In this way, the sliced pieces will not stick together, and they will have more interesting shapes.

Cutting is most important because it determines the appearance of the dish and the length of time the food should be cooked. There are various ways of cutting: fairly large in cubes of about 1½ inches suitable for stewing and braising; sliced, shredded, diced and minced for sautéeing. By slices we mean pieces 1½ inches long by 1 inch wide and about ⅟₁₆ of an inch thick. Shreds have one dimension less than slices, therefore, when we mention shreds we mean pieces 1½ inches long with hardly any width or thickness. By dicing we mean the cutting of the ingredient into any cubelike size you wish. A Chinese cook prefers to mince his meat with a cleaver rather than with a grinder, because he feels that putting the meat through the workout of cleavers draws out and retains the juice.

The method of cutting is determined first by the nature of the ingredients and second by the appearance of the other dishes. All food should be cut into the same size in the same dish. If you are cooking chicken with peas, dice the chicken. If you are going to cook the chicken with bean sprouts, cut the chicken in strips the same length as the sprouts. Variety, they say, is the spice of life and it is no less so in the Chinese kitchen. If the ingredients in one dish are prepared in fine strips, it would be more interesting to have the ingredients in the second diced.

Food cut into small pieces cooks quickly and is easy to season. These two principles account for the distinctive taste of Chinese food. All Chinese food is cooked thoroughly but yet remains wholesome. Very little water is added in the cooking, since the method of quick frying brings out the natural juices from the food. This liquid makes enough sauce for the dish and is very tasty. Nothing is more abhorrent to a gourmet than to find a dish slopped over with a sauce composed of water and a thickening agent.

If different ingredients in the same dish take different lengths of time to cook, each ingredient should be put in at the right time so that all come out done together. That is the technique of good sautéeing. When the meat is the principal ingredient in the dish, the proportion should be about three fifths of meat to two fifths of the vegetable. Should there be more than one accompanying ingredient, be sure that the principal ingredient outweighs all the accompaniments combined.

When the meat and the vegetables are combined in one dish, they are cooked separately first, since the main ingredients are cooked under different conditions. The vegetable should be cooked first, since it does it no harm to wait for the final cooking. Oil the pan (preferably with peanut oil but any vegetable oil except olive oil will do), and, when it is very hot, add the vegetable and sauté for about one minute, or just until the vegetable turns bright green. The pan should be very hot, otherwise the vegetable will become limp. Take the vegetable out of the pan and set it aside. Now heat the pan again with a little oil and, when it is very hot, add the meat and sauté till it is three-quarters done, that is while the meat is still red. Add the vegetable and continue to sauté for about thirty seconds more, and then add the seasoning. If the pan gets too dry, add a little more oil down the side of the pan, not on the food. The meat and vegetable should be stirred constantly. The vegetable will give out juice, so very little water need be added. However, should a recipe call for water, it should be hot unless otherwise specified. Liquid seasoning such as soy sauce and sherry should not be added too early. Cooking meat in liquid will toughen it. Liquids should only be added when the meat slices are half-done and then it should be poured on part of the hot pan and not mixed with the ingredients till it is heated. Pepper, salt and other seasonings are added just before the dish is ready. Chinese chefs always add sugar to their cooking—they believe that it brings out the flavor of the food. It also goes in at this time. All these are general rules; there are many exceptions as you will note in the recipes, but if you wish to make up a recipe of your own, it would be a good idea to follow them.

The liquid (which includes soy sauce, wine and other juices

accumulated during cooking) may be thickened with cornstarch just before serving, but this is not necessary and often not desirable. Take the pan off the fire just as the vegetable is turning a darker green and the meat is still undercooked, as they will continue to cook in the hot pan even when off the fire.

A hot fire is essential in sautéeing. The Chinese frying pan or *kuo* (but known in this country as wok) has rounded sides. This allows every part of it to become very hot, making it superior to an ordinary frying pan for this method of cooking.

Chinese food must be served very hot, especially fish and sautéed dishes; therefore, never start to sauté till everyone is seated. Peanut oil is recommended for sautéeing meat dishes, but lard is preferred for plain vegetables.

Vegetables may be parboiled beforehand if you wish to save time at the last minute. Pass the vegetable through boiling water and, when it turns bright green, take it out and plunge it briefly into cold water in order to retain the color. Set this aside. The vegetable is now ready to be cooked with the meat.

❋ Red Cooking or Hung Shao

Red cooking is a type of stewing with soy sauce known as *hung shao*. *Hung* means red, and the soy sauce gives the juice a reddish color. Very often it is necessary to brown the meat first. Pork shoulder, stew beef, chicken, duck and carp are well suited to the *hung shao* method. This takes one to six hours of cooking depending on the size of the cut of meat.

❋ Deep Frying

Deep frying is another common way of cooking in China. Cut meat into medium-sized pieces; and if fish is to be served whole, deep gashes on the sides should be made. Marinate the meat in soy sauce, sherry and other seasoning for about half an hour, and then fry in deep fat. Pieces of meat and fish may be dipped in a mixture of egg and flour and then deep-fried. This may be served with a pepper-and-salt mixture.

✳ Steaming

Steaming is a favorite method of cooking à la Chinoise, especially for fresh-water fish. There are two kinds of steaming, wet and dry. Western cooks usually employ the method of dry steaming in a double boiler in which the steam never actually touches the food. Chinese cooks wet-steam their food and that is why they have tiers of perforated partitions in their steamers. Steaming fish is the best way of preserving its delicate texture and taste. The plate should be heated before the fish is placed in it. And the water in the utensil must be steaming before the plate is placed in that. This is very important, because if the plate is not hot, and the water not steaming, the fish will be just sitting there the first few minutes, getting heated but not cooked. As soon as the fish is put in the steaming vessel, place the cover on the vessel and turn up the heat so that the steam is at its height. Serve the fish just undercooked, as the heat from the fish will finish the cooking while on the table. In recipes that call for steaming, food should be wet-steamed, Chinese style.

✳ Roasting, Barbecuing or Grilling

The mode of cooking least used in China is roasting and barbecuing, because fuel is expensive and hard to get. The typical Chinese oven for roasting is open, and the cooking is usually done on a spit. This is a very familiar sight to Americans today, with their outdoor barbecues and rotisseries.

There is very little boiling per se in the Chinese cuisine. However, to make clear soup, the Chinese employ a slow simmering process. As soon as the boiling starts, the fire should be turned low and the liquid allowed to simmer for a considerable length of time. No soy sauce is added. When poultry is cooked whole and is to be eaten with the soup, there are two ways of cooking it. If it is more important to have good soup, the chicken should be put in cold water. If it is more important to have a tasty chicken, then it should be put in boiling water. This rule also applies to meat which is to be cooked the same way.

Meats for making soup vary in taste according to how they are treated. When meat slices are undercooked, the result will be a tasty soup and tender meat. If the meat is a little overcooked, the soup will remain tasty but the meat will no longer be tender. When the meat is greatly overcooked, the soup will remain tasty but the meat will be barely palatable.

✳ General Hints

Everything, of course, has to be cleaned, and we take that for granted. In China, rice used to be washed in rice baskets—this lets the water run through, yet the web is small enough to prevent the grains from washing away. Rice baskets are not easy to get in the United States, so for our purposes the rice may be washed in two changes of water.

Dried ingredients should be soaked in cold water till they soften, then cleaned and then resoaked in hot water till very soft. When they are soft, take them out of the liquor and drain and cut as directed. The seasoned water should be kept and used when liquid is called for in that particular dish.

Ginger is found in varying sizes, so when we specify a piece of ginger we mean one the size of a walnut. A slice of ginger should be about ⅛-inch thick and the diameter of a walnut. To facilitate the chopping or slicing of such slippery ingredients as ginger, clove of garlic and scallions, press down on them with the flat side of the cleaver until they rest firmly on the cutting board.

Substitute American vegetables when Chinese ones are not available. Cook them the Chinese way and you will have an authentic Chinese dish with an Oriental flavor. Longer-cooking vegetables, such as onions, green peppers and celery, naturally would go into the pan first. Tender vegetables, such as spinach, would go in last.

Cooking time is given in the recipes but the degree of heat is the controlling factor, so it is most important to keep your eye on the food. With practice, the experienced cook will be able to judge when a dish is ready. As a general rule, it is better to under-cook than overcook—that is, everything except pork.

In a Chinese meal the food is served at the table ready to be eaten. It is always previously cut or prepared in such a way that a knife is not necessary at table.

Cutting roast poultry Chinese style is an art unto itself, and with practice comes perfection. Here is how it is usually done in a Chinese kitchen. Remove legs and wings and chop them into 1-inch pieces. Cut the chicken in half through the backbone. Cut the halves of the chicken into 5 or 6 pieces and then arrange on a serving dish skin side upward with the wings and the legs.

"Prevention is better than cure" applies also to cooking, but in the event you have put too much vinegar in a dish, add salt to correct the taste. If it is too salty, add a little sugar and vinegar; too cloying, add salt; and should the dish be too bland, add monosodium glutamate. Except in complete vegetable dishes and few other exceptions, this is the only time the author recom-mends the use of this taste powder. Good cooks in China very seldom use monosodium glutamate because its flavor too often masks careless cooking.

It is difficult to say just how many people a given recipe will serve. In Chinese meals, if there are more people more different dishes are prepared instead of making one dish in larger quantity. In this book, we have given the amounts needed for four people when four dishes and a soup are served. The exceptions to this rule are the dishes prepared from large pieces of meat, such as pork shoulder; whole poultry, such as turkey and duck; and whole fish, such as carp. Chungking watermelon soup and winter melon soup are also exceptions, but as a general rule, the author has tried to give proportions for four people when four dishes are served. If you have five people at the table add another dish. But if that is not practicable, then increase the proportion of the main dish, or choose one of the large dishes, such as a whole duck.

We have tried to give the Wade-Giles spelling of the mandarin or *Kuo yu* (national language) for the names of dishes in this book. Many of the dishes are varied in nature, as they have been collected from the far corners of China. Friends and relatives who were good enough to give them to me knew only the local designations, and we have tried to translate them into the equivalent in the national language. Many of you may know better and may smile at our efforts, but we beg your indulgence.

UTENSILS

Old Chinese stoves were built of concrete, tiles and brick and were conical in shape with the opening on top. In a large kitchen, there would be many of these openings. The stove was considered part of the house and built in when the house was built. At night the flames were banked, and the next morning the cinders and ashes were removed and the fire was fanned up. For the poorer people and those who were not able to have such large kitchens, portable stoves known as *chatties* were devised. They were made of baked clay on the same principle as the large immovable stove, and were fed with wood and charcoal.

Although many houses retained the old-style stove, with the advent of modern conveniences most homes in the large cities of China were also equipped with electric and gas stoves. Gas was more popular than electricity for Chinese stoves, because with gas the flame can be controlled instantly.

There are many things which catch the eye as soon as you enter a Chinese kitchen. First is the cooking utensil known in this country as a wok, but called a *kuo* in China. It is a cooking pan with rounded bottom which allows for even heat and has no corners to make removal of food awkward. Cast-iron woks are preferable to aluminum ones. You can use this vessel for sautéeing, for cooking with either small or large amounts of water, for deep frying and as the base for a steamer. Fill the pan with water and place tiers of bamboo baskets above it, and you have a most useful utensil. It is used for pastry, steamed fish and custards. If you cannot get these bamboo steamers, use a rack and cover the *kuo*, and this receptacle will function as a steamer. A double-boiler type of pot may be used for a steamer also, but the bottom of the top saucepan must be perforated to allow the steam to circulate around the food; or a rack may be placed in a saucepan so as to suspend the food above the water in the pan.

A vegetable cutting knife known as a *ch'ieh-tsai tao* is indispensable in a Chinese kitchen. With it, you can chop bones, scale fish and mince meat. Cleavers of varying sizes should be kept in a well-appointed kitchen. Sharp heavy knives such as these should be employed so that the weight of the metal will do most of the work, rather than your strength exerted upon a small, light knife. With a heavy knife there is no need to saw back and forth across the food. A pair of knives of equal size should be used for mincing. They should be about 3 inches wide and 6 to 8 inches long. The blunt edge at the top of the blade is anywhere from $\frac{1}{16}$ to $\frac{1}{8}$ of an inch wide. The edge of the blade should be kept sharp at all times. These knives take the place of food chopper, potato masher, onion mincer, steak cuber, various-sized graters, paring knife, bread knife and steak knife.

The most picturesque thing that you see in the Chinese kitchen is the chopping block. It is about 5 or 6 inches thick and is cut from the trunk of the soap tree (*sapindus saponario*). To be really useful it should be about 16 to 18 inches in diameter. The soap tree is a tropical growth that has a wonderful patina and pretty grain. If this cannot be procured, any wooden chopping block will do, but the thicker the better.

A large cutting board is a necessity in a Chinese kitchen. This is the same as those found in most American kitchens. Since noodles, *hun t'un* and *pao tzu* are made at home, this type of board is most useful. The Chinese rolling pin is a simple roller 1½ inches in diameter and from 8 to 30 inches long.

A utensil like a pancake turner is important in a kitchen like this. The blade ought to be about 3 inches square. Try not to get one with a long blade, for the smaller the blade the easier it is to control. Wooden dippers are used for water and liquids, and china spoons and wooden chopsticks are used for stirring and tasting, for the Chinese do not like to handle raw food with metal. Colanders and sieves are useful utensils in the Chinese kitchen. Earthenware pots are a necessity; they are similar to the casseroles used by the French. These are good for the slow cooking required for "red cooking," steaming and simmering.

Chopsticks are the utensils one uses for eating. They are made of silver, ivory, bamboo, wood or plastic. They are about 10 inches long and about the thickness of a pencil or a little thinner. These two pieces of wood take the place of egg beaters, cooking forks, mixing spoons, draining spoons and wire whisks. It's no wonder a Chinese cook cannot do without them, for they rarely break, never go out of commission and are very easy to keep clean.

With the advent of modern utensils, Chinese cooks have advanced with the times too. No good cooking should be hurried, but if you are in haste, a pressure cooker is the answer. For those of you who live in a high altitude it is essential. My brother and sister-in-law live at about 11,000 feet and they use a pressure cooker even for rice. But for us at sea level the advantage of a pressure cooker is for "red cooking," and for other dishes which require a long cooking time. As a general rule use a 15-pound pressure and 20 minutes pressurized time. After you turn off the heat, let the cooker stand for about half an hour to let the color and flavor of the seasoning seep into the food. Shoulder of pork or pot roast should be left standing at least one hour—longer if the meat cut is very large. The pressure cooker is especially good for foods with sauce, but you must never more than half fill the pot as rising liquids may clog the vent.

Chinese dinner service is fashioned out of either silver or porcelain and is made in various shapes. Often these shapes are derived from various fruits, such as peaches, gourds and pomegranates. The largest porcelain manufacturing city is Ching Te Chen, near Kiukiang. One hundred and forty-eight pieces of china make up a table service for ten, but many pieces could be eliminated. Each setting consists of many pieces. A medium-sized plate about the size of a saucer is the central piece. A smaller condiment dish is placed to the upper right, and next to it is placed a small bowl about 2½ inches in diameter. This is for the soup and is called, in my province, the almond tea bowl. The rice bowl is about 3½ inches in diameter and is placed on the plate. The wine cup is a little larger than a thimble and is usually kept filled with warm rice wine. A porcelain spoon on its stand and a pair of chopsticks complete the table setting. In some homes, silver or porcelain chopstick rests are used.

Chinese food should be served in the Chinese way, and Chinese dishes are better designed for this purpose than Western style dishes. Vessels for soup have straight sides like the French soufflé dishes. Besides the table setting, it would be well to have the following dishes for serving: four large shallow bowls, four large round plates, two deep bowls, two round covered soup dishes, two long platters for fish, various-sized porcelain spoons for serving, small condiment dishes for mustard, soy sauce, pepper and salt and ten special individual soup bowls for sharks' fins.

ETIQUETTE
AND CUSTOMS

When we were living in China, most of the Chinese had three main meals a day, except for those who lived in the south and west. The first meal of the day was of soft rice, or congee as it is known to Westerners in the Orient. This is a kind of porridge, made of rice instead of oatmeal. Dishes of salty or savory foods, such as salted peanuts, salt vegetables and scrambled eggs, or as in my province of Fukien, *jo sung*, a kind of mincemeat made of pork, were served with this gruel. Hard or dry rice was the staple at lunch and dinner. The dishes varied for each meal and the same dish was never served twice on the same day.

In Kwangtung and the lands adjoining to the west, they had two main meals a day at the times of day when the rest of China did not. These two meals were the same as our lunch and dinner, and the majority of the Cantonese used to follow this meal system. However, those who were wealthy and had more leisure were served two large meals and three smaller ones in between. These smaller meals are known as *tien hsins,* and have become very famous outside the province of Kwangtung. In fact, these *tien hsins* have become so famous that they are now served as main meals to foreigners in the many Chinatowns of the world.

The wealthier Cantonese used to make a light repast on congee when they got up in the morning, say at about seven. Later, at about ten-thirty, they would have their regular meal with rice, and at one-thirty or two, they would take assorted steamed pastries, egg rolls and the like. At five or six in the evening they had their second big meal, and then, before they retired, a delicious bowl of noodles or congee cooked with chicken or fish was served.

Many Americans who have only been bidden to the festive board do not realize that there is anything besides a banquet in the Chinese manner of dining, but in reality there are two distinct ways of serving meals—the family meal and the party meal. The dishes may be the same, but the mode of serving is different.

In a family meal, or when there are about six people present, some five dishes and a soup will be placed in the middle of the table and a bowl of rice served to each diner. Each person will help himself to the dishes, a little at a time. The dishes in the center are never passed, and for this reason a round table is most convenient. One does not fill the small plate in front of himself and eat exclusively from that. No, a Chinese meal is much more sociable than that. The bowl of rice in front of you is for yourself alone, but you share the dishes in the middle of the table, and it is not considered good manners to take the tenderest morsel yourself. Someone else at the table will pick out a dainty and put it on your plate for you!

In the old days, when one gave a dinner party, one sent around a messenger with written invitations and a receipt book. The recipients, in signing the book, could see who the other guests were, and therefore could come prepared to meet a friend or the "lion" of the moment, or decline the invitation if the presence of some guest would be embarrassing to them. We would never have found ourselves in the predicament most of the diplomatic corps fell into when we were in Copenhagen. At the time we were living in Denmark, there were countless divorces and remarriages. Many of our friends had married so many times that we couldn't remember who the ex-husbands and ex-wives were, and if we did, we didn't know or didn't remember whether they were on good terms or not—and very often wives number one, two and three met at the same dinner or reception. In China, this would never have happened; if the host didn't know the situation, the guests themselves were given ample warning, and they would have acted as circumstances dictated.

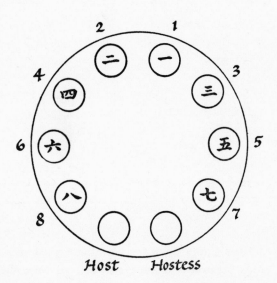

The seating at a Chinese banquet is completely different from the Western way. The host and hostess sit together with their backs to the door, which usually opens to the south, and those who sit next to them occupy the lowliest seats. The seats of honor are those opposite the host and hostess, facing the door, the right side of the guest of honor being lowlier than the left, and so on until the lowliest seat is found on the left side of the host. In the old yamen and courtyards, direction was most important and the highest seats faced south. In the more modern houses, where architects were not so strict regarding direction, the seat facing the door was considered the highest. This was so because in the Manchu days the Emperor was known as the Son of Heaven and his throne was always placed on the north side of the hall facing south.

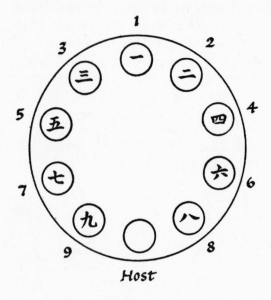

Host

The dining table for a Chinese meal is generally round, not only because it places each diner at the same distance from the center where the food is placed, but because mealtimes among Chinese are a time of relaxation and of pleasantry and a round table is better for general conversation.

Chopsticks in Chinese are called *k'uai tzu*, which means "quick little ones." "Quick" in that awful language known as pidgin English is "chop"—hence the name chopsticks came into being. Usually they are made of silver, ivory or bamboo. Ivory and bamboo are the commonest and bamboo the easiest to manage.

The top half is squared and the bottom half, rounded. The host and hostess often have extra pairs of chopsticks, which may or may not be extra long, to pass special delicacies to the guests. Spare chopsticks and place settings are never left at the table; they are removed before the guests are seated.

When a guest has finished eating, he will hold his chopsticks together, point them downward, graciously make a gesture to the others at the table and put them on his bowl, which indicates that although he has finished eating, he wants you to take your time and enjoy your meal.

Although it is not considered polite to finish the dishes in the center of the table, one should always eat every grain of rice in his bowl. The custom probably stems from the fact that grain is the staff of life and therefore not to be wasted.

The Western host always brags about his good dishes, but a Chinese host must deprecate his food. My father has lived abroad so long, having been with Westerners since the age of sixteen, that he often forgets these little niceties. I remember once when he was a host at a party in China he kept telling the guests how wonderful each dish was, till his younger sister could stand it no longer and chided him in the tongue of their childhood. "Brother, have you been abroad so long that you've forgotten that we never say that our own food is good?" Daddy replied to her in an undertone, and in the secret language of Foochow: "I cannot understand why we have to say it's bad—it seems so rude to invite guests to eat bad food!" So ideas do change with change of environment.

The Chinese are nondrinkers as a rule. And when they do drink, it is at a banquet where custom, food and etiquette demand it. Anyone who drinks alone and not at mealtime is a rarity.

At a party, as each dish is placed on the table, either the host lifts his cup and bids the guests drink, or a guest may toast the host and thank him for his party. As there is an interval between dishes, the party is made somewhat livelier by a game played by two known as *Hua chuan* or matching fingers. This game was invented to sharpen the faculties. You have to have all your wits about you to play it well. The two players face each other with their right forearms raised and elbows resting on the table. At a signal given mutually, the hand and forearm of each player is thrown forward with a number of fingers extended or with clenched fists. The object of the game is to guess the correct number of the sum of fingers shown. It is quite fascinating to watch and listen to expert players, for they play in perfect synchronization with chanted rhymes.

To emphasize the fact that drinking is not considered one of the enviable pleasures of China, it is the loser at this fingers game who is penalized and made to drink a cup of wine. In the event that the same person persistently loses, the winner, to soften the blow, will drink with the loser.

There is one custom which my mother didn't like, but which the Westerners in China loved and took to readily. I refer to the hot towels. Instead of table napkins, each guest is handed a steaming towel to wipe his hands and his mouth before and after the meal. It is most refreshing, especially after having partaken of anything sticky.

When the meal comes to an end, it is the guest of honor who makes the first move. Slowly, the other guests follow suit and the host leaves the table last.

TEAS
AND WINES

There are various legends and stories as to how tea was either discovered in or introduced to China. The one most quoted is that about the Emperor Sheng Nung who lived in 2737 B.C. The Emperor, even at that early date, was interested in hygiene. He had noticed that people who drank boiled water enjoyed better health than those who did not, so he decreed that all his subjects drink boiled water. One day while he was in the woods, his henchmen made a fire with the branches of an old tree. As the water boiled, "two leaves and a bud" of the withered tree fell into the boiling water and imparted a delightful aroma. Sheng Nung sipped the liquid and enjoyed it, and ever since then tea has been synonymous with China.

There are three main types of tea produced in China: green, black (known as red among the Chinese) and *oolung*. The leaves all come from the same plant, but they are processed differently. To produce green tea, the leaves are plucked before they are withered and are given a quicker drying period than the black tea. Because of less handling, the leaves look and taste more like the original plant, therefore the smaller and more tender leaves on top of the tree are used for green tea. The leaves look green-gray in color when processed and are given exotic grade names starting with the finest: Young Hysen, Hysen Numbers 1 and 2, Gunpowder, Twankey, Fannings and Dust. The leaves of the Hysen types are rolled lengthwise.

To make black tea, the leaves are withered first and then go through a special process which changes the chemical composition through the absorption of oxygen. This oxidation changes the color of the leaves. I have been asked very often about the fancy names on boxes of tea that a word here would not be amiss. There are two general grade classifications—Broken and Leaf. The former is made up of the smaller leaves sifted from the main bulk of tea. The latter represents the large leaves left from the sifting of the broken grade. The leaf types are divided into these grade names: Orange Pekoe, Pekoe, Pekoe Souchong. The broken grades are subdivided into Broken Orange Pekoe, Broken Pekoe, Broken Pekoe Souchong, Fannings and Dust. These terms denote the size and appearance of the leaves and have no reference to quality or kind. Broken grades normally give darker liquor and stronger tea, but darkness does not always denote strength. Leaf grades are lighter in color and the tea is weaker. The word Pekoe is an erroneous phonetic translation by the early tea merchants of the Chinese words meaning "white hairs." The tea was thus designated because the early pickings of tea leaves had white down on them. Many varieties of tea are scented with fragrant flowers, hence a name such as Orange Pekoe.

Oolung tea is a cross between green and black tea. The leaves are partly fermented. Most of it is produced in Formosa, although some is found on the mainland. It was given this name, which means black dragon, because of the appearance of the leaves after curing. However, as with everything else in China, there is a legend surrounding this name. Centuries ago a Chinese from my province of Fukien migrated to Formosa. One day, while he was picking tea in his garden, he noticed a fragrance emanating from a certain tree. Upon closer examination, he saw a beautiful black serpent intertwined among the branches. Taking this as a good omen, he made a brew of the leaves of the tree and found it good. In honor of the beautiful snake he called the tea Black Dragon. *Oolung* tea leaves, being partly processed, are partly brown and partly green and the liquid is bright in color.

The tea tree is an evergreen of the camellia family and is grown from seed. It grows in a hot, moist climate. The first harvesting takes place three or four years after planting, and after that the leaves may be picked every three or four months. The leaf is plucked at the time of its most active growth, known as the flush period. Usually women do the plucking, as they have a lighter hand. Sixty pounds per day is considered a good day's work per person. It takes four pounds of freshly plucked leaves to make one pound of tea.

The first tea to be exported to Britain was from the port of Amoy in Fukien Province. The name for this beverage in the local dialect was *tay*. Slowly the word was corrupted till it was finally known as tea. In Mandarin the word for tea is *ch'a*. It is interesting to note that a word which sounds like *ch'a* is used in Russian to denote this beverage.

The flavor of the tea is attributed to the different environments in which the plant grows and the methods of preparation. Very often there are over twenty varieties of leaves in one blend. According to some tea tasters, it is practically impossible to mix a bad blend of tea as long as you have good tea leaves to work with, while it takes an expert to blend good coffee even if you have the best coffee beans at your disposal. Leaves of flowers such as jasmine, chrysanthemums and camellias often add fragrance.

The best green tea comes from Hangchow in the district known as Lung-ching, which means Dragon Well. As this green tea has become so famous, the word "Lung-ching" has become synonymous with green tea, although much of it comes from Southern

Anhwei. Hangchow also produces *oolung* tea which is made from the semi-fermented leaves. When jasmine is mixed with it, it is known as jasmine tea. But one type of tea which is most prized in China is the T'ieh Kuang-yin, or Iron Goddess, which comes from the province of Fukien. It is a black tea and most fragrant. Keemun is also a black tea and comes from Yünnan.

Tea is a delicate plant which readily absorbs flavor and moisture. It should, therefore, not be exposed to the air, but kept in an airtight canister. After a certain period of time tea loses its fragrance; it should not be kept longer than six months.

We Chinese attach much importance to the shape and material of the pot in the making of good tea. A china pot is preferred, as we feel that metal ones impart a foreign flavor. We like them flat and round in shape because a tall pot exposes the tea leaves to only a very small area of water.

There are five golden rules for making good tea. The first and most obvious one is that tea leaves should be of the finest. Second, the water should be freshly drawn and freshly boiled. The water should not be allowed to boil after boiling point is reached, as that drives the oxygen from the water and the tea tastes flat. Be sure that the teapot has been preheated. Since the water should be at the highest boil when it touches the tea leaves, the teapot should be taken to the boiling water and not the boiling water to the pot. And last but not least, the tea should be brewed from three to five minutes and not stewed for a longer length of time.

It is important to see that the water is at a rolling boil before trying to infuse the tea. If the water is not rolling, half of the tea leaves in the pot will float and remain floating during the whole infusion. The rest will stay at the bottom from the beginning, and there will be very little movement of leaves. What movement there is will be from bottom to top and the flavor of the beverage will be very poor.

Tea made with freshly boiling water will have two thirds of the leaves floating at the start of the infusion. The tea leaves on the bottom will rise to the top and those from the top will sink. The movement will be very marked. In five minutes, all the leaves will have sunk to the bottom and the result will be a brew with good body and good flavor.

If water is boiled too long, the leaves will sink to the bottom from the start of the infusion. The brew will be thin, the flavor poor and lacking in character.

China tea is very fragrant and is much stronger than it looks. Green tea should be only pale yellow in color to be at its best. If it is any stronger, it will taste like a herbalist brew. Individual taste should govern how strong one wants to make tea. One teaspoon of tea leaves per cup and one for the pot still holds good for some teas, and you can always rectify strong tea by watering it down, but you cannot do anything about strengthening weak tea. But for green tea and many other China teas, one heaping teaspoon to six cups of water makes a very fragrant drink. With this type of tea, one does not desecrate it by adding sugar and milk. It should be taken pure. However, if you find it impossible to take tea without some sweetening, choose a tea brewed with sweet-smelling flowers such as chrysanthemums. Rock sugar added to this type of tea would be permissible.

After the contents of the pot are reduced, more freshly made boiling water should be added with good Chinese tea, the second infusion is often thought to be the better, and with fastidious drinkers, the first quick infusion is thrown away and the second one inhaled and enjoyed like brandy.

As a general rule, tea is not served during mealtimes in Chinese homes, except in parts of Fukien and eastern Kwangtung. (Since the first restaurants in the United States were opened by Cantonese, their custom was thought to be typically Chinese.) In homes and at formal occasions, tea is served in traditional teacups. The set is made in three parts—the handleless cup, a saucer and a cover. The tea leaves are brewed in the cup, and the tea is taken from the cup with the lid on.

Tea is so much a part of Chinese life that a story is woven around it. The tea plant cannot, after maturity, be moved without dying, so it symbolizes fidelity, and a gift of tea means friendship. Among the presents sent to a girl's family on the occasion of her engagement, there is sure to be some very fine tea.

Although we have been talking about tea as the Chinese take it, let us see how iced tea came to this country. A young Englishman by the name of Richard Blenchynden was sent to the St. Louis Exposition to represent Indian and Ceylon teas. He had with him some Singhalese assistants wearing colorful turbans, and his booth was exotic indeed. At any other time, it would have attracted scores of visitors. But the weather was stifling hot, and when people saw the steaming tea, they hurried past to where the iced drinks were sold. Day after day this went on, till the young Englishman became desperate. He gritted his teeth and said to himself that if the Americans wanted iced drinks he would supply them; so he filled his glasses with ice and poured tea over it. The golden brew looked tempting, and before the fair closed, the cooling and refreshing drink had become so popular that its fame spread far and wide and it is now a national summer drink.

A Chinese discovered tea, an Englishman invented iced tea, but it remained for an American to put it in a form to popularize the merchandising of it among his fellow Americans.

Thomas Sullivan owned a wholesale tea and coffee business. Every year he sent samples in tins to his customers. But he found these tins most expensive, so he ordered hundreds of silk bags to be made. These he filled with tea and sent them to his customers. To his surprise orders flowed in, not for his tea alone, but for the new way it was packaged. His customers had discovered the convenience of making tea with bags that could be easily disposed of.

* Wines

The wines of China are not made from grapes but are distilled from *kaoliang* (a kind of millet), rice and other cereals; the use of the word "wine" may therefore be erroneous. But as it has been known as such through the years, we shall continue to use the word to simplify matters.

In north China, where *kaoliang* grew in abundance, the liquor was distilled from that grain. It was stronger than either vodka and gin, though reminiscent of them. In central China, the wine was distilled from rice. The best came from the district of Hsiao-hsing in Chekiang Province and took its name from the city in which it was manufactured. As it was amber in color, it was often referred to as *huang-chiu*, "yellow wine." These wines are taken warm and served from porcelain, silver or pewter pots.

Pilots of the American Volunteer Group (which later became known as the famous Flying Tigers), while they were in Kunming and Chungking, tried a strong white spirit distilled from corn and known as *pai-kan*. It was so strong that they promptly dubbed it "white lightning."

In past years, much has been discovered through accident. There is a story, which has been discounted, regarding a monk in France who is supposed to have inadvertently made champagne. In China, we also have such a legend regarding rice wine, but so far the story has not been disproved.

Centuries ago, so the story goes, a cook in the imperial kitchen in Peking left some rice to soak in a crock. He forgot about it for many days. When he came across it again, he took a spoonful of the liquid to see if the precious grain had been spoiled. When he tasted the liquid, he found it good and took some more. Upon imbibing more and more of it, he became exhilarated and quite light-headed. His daily chores seemed to become lighter, and the world not nearly as drab as it used to be.

His find was reported to the Emperor, who sampled it in turn. He agreed with his chef that he had indeed discovered something remarkable. His duties did not seem so heavy, and it wasn't nearly so boring to talk to his ministers after he had had a couple of bowls of this liquid.

Just about this time, the Emperor was preparing to welcome his councilors, the nobles of his kingdom and foreign envoys at a state dinner. He decided to serve his new-found elixir of life to them. He wanted to share with them the liquid which made all burdens lighter. He ordered the cooks in the palace to make him vats of this concoction. And for days in the courtyards of the imperial palace, nothing could be seen but the large earthenware vats filled with the intoxicating liquid.

The subsequent dinner was a magnificent affair and most successful—as far as the Emperor was concerned. Ministers and councilors, who previously had not seen eye to eye with the Emperor, agreed to his every suggestion. The foreign envoys, too, were willing to grant him his every wish. In short, the wine did its work well.

In this period of history, the Son of Heaven always used to hold his audiences early in the morning before sunrise, as it was thought that men's minds were more alert at that time. The morning after this banquet, the Emperor sat on his Dragon Throne awaiting his councilors of state, but he waited in vain. Not one of them turned up. They had been overpowered by the rice wine. Messengers from the imperial palace were dispatched to wake them and bid them come, but alas, no amount of shaking could rouse them. The messengers returned, fearing for their heads, and all announced that the councilors to a man were drugged.

This set the Emperor to pondering. He did not think the wine bad—if taken in moderation. But how to ensure that his ministers did not repeat their indiscretion? After due thought, he decreed that the soup bowls in which wine had been served the night before were too big. In their stead he ordered tiny thimble-sized cups to be made for wine, which are in use to this day. He also commanded that wine must be taken with small tidbits of solid food, that no one was to drink on an empty stomach—and that was the origin of the leng pen, "cold dish" or hors d'oeuvres. And so that the imbiber would not take too much of the wine cup, and so that there would be an interval between drinks, the Emperor insisted that a game be played at table. In order to be able to play well, they had to have their wits about them, and so the game of *Hua chuan* was invented. Since that early date, the Chinese have tried to keep to these three rules, and I must say that the results have been successful, as it is a rare thing indeed to see a Chinese intoxicated.

We have heard so much regarding the welcome a male child receives when he arrives in a Chinese home, that it is refreshing to relate that when a daughter makes her debut into a family, it is the custom to make as much wine as possible in her honor. These bottles are put away for twenty-odd years, to be served on her wedding day.

Aged wines are the best, and a forty-year-old wine is considered very good indeed, but wines which are only a few years old are also palatable. However, it is difficult for us living in America to get rice wine, so we have to find substitutes for it. Red wines and rosés as a rule do not go well with a Chinese dinner, except with heavy dishes such as duck in a thick gravy. Sherry is similar to Chinese rice wine, but for some it may seem a bit heavy. However, many Chinese serve this when rice wine is not available. White wine goes well with Chinese food, especially if it is very dry. The French wine which goes best with Chinese dishes is a Graves and for those who prefer domestic products, the white California premium wines are good.

The liqueurs of China are also distilled from grains such as *kaoliang* and corn. They are colored and flavored with peach, melon, orange, rose petals, lotus flowers and other fragrances. A good example of this is the *Mei Kwei Lu*, a strong, colorless liquid flavored with rose petals.

FESTIVALS, SUPERSTITIONS AND SYMBOLS

When we lived in China the festival days were joyous ones for everyone concerned. They were looked forward to by all of us, just as Christmas is by all of you in this country.

There are many festivals observed throughout the year, but the three main ones are the Chinese New Year, the Dragon Boat Festival and the Moon Festival. The dates vary from year to year and are determined by the moon. New Year's Day falls on the second new moon after the winter solstice. Americans are aware of this festival because of the dragon parades which take place in the Chinatowns of various large cities in the United States.

✳ *Chinese New Year*

For about a fortnight before New Year's Day, Ah Hing used to keep my mother's kitchen buzzing as he prepared enough food to last the first three days of the New Year, when no one was expected to work. His creations for the first day of the year were simple compared with the New Year's Eve fare. Everything was prepared and ready to be warmed up. In many homes, only food which needed no cutting was served, but we did not carry the observance to such extremes, although we looked on the first day of the year as the root of the future and, therefore, one which should be started well.

New Year's Eve is a great day for us, for we believe it is as essential to end the year well as it is to begin it auspiciously. In our family home, as in most homes in China, the ancestral tablets were kept on the altar. On the last day of the year, we would light red candles and set a full dinner on the low table near the altar for the souls of the departed. This Ah Hing prepared and served as lovingly as if the departed souls actually could appreciate the excellence of his art. Chinese are a practical people, and—not surprisingly—he would serve these same dishes to the living members of the family that night. The married members of the family all try to return home for this last meal of the year, and this dinner is in a way the Chinese equivalent of the fatted calf.

At midnight, all the shops used to close and no business was transacted. All debts should be paid by midnight on this last day of the year, and everyone is ready to start the new year with a clean slate.

When we were in China, our family, like others, used to hold open house on New Year's Day. Friends came to call and to wish us a Happy and Prosperous New Year. We of the younger generation used to call on our elders and pay our respects. In return, they plied us with sweetmeats and delicacies, each one being some sort of symbol: a fresh green olive, an ingot of gold; a tangerine, happiness; watermelon seeds, fertility; and lotus seeds, male issue. Dragon's eyes, a kind of fruit, symbolize something precious. Children and unmarried girls receive red envelopes containing money, and no harsh words or unkind thoughts are allowed to prevail. This goes on for about three to five days, till slowly life goes back to normal at about the end of the first week.

✳ Dragon Boat Festival

The Dragon Boat Festival falls on the fifth day of the fifth moon and is also called the Double Fifth. The origin of the festival goes back to the fourth century B.C. There is a story of Chu Yuan, a wise official whom the King of Chu appointed as one of his councilors. Because of the King's partiality, the other ministers became jealous of Chu Yuan and vilified him until the King believed their stories and exiled Chu Yuan to south China. He disguised himself as a fisherman but continued to write poems in which he tried to warn the King of the corruption of the court. He had no success and became very despondent, and on the fifth day of the fifth moon, he drowned himself. After Chu's death, the King realized Chu's loyalty and he so grieved that he vowed to look after the spirit of Chu Yuan. He thereupon ordered *chung tzu* to be thrown into the river where Chu had drowned. *Chung tzu* are boiled packets of glutinous rice studded with jujubes, meat or red beans wrapped in bamboo leaves. For centuries after, dragon boats raced on this river and *chung tzu* were thrown into the water to sustain the spirit of Chu Yuan. And on this day, in memory of Chu Yuan, we eat these rice dumplings.

✳ The Moon Festival

The third big holiday is the Moon Festival which falls on the fifteenth day of the eighth moon, known as the Harvest Moon in this country. The most popular story about this festival originated in the twenty-fifth century B.C. It tells the story of Chang Ngo, wife of an alchemist. One day during the fall of the year, Chang Ngo stole three pills from her husband and swallowed them. Her husband had spent his whole life in making them. He was hoping to discover the secret of preserving life and of making humans into divinities. When the husband discovered the theft he flew into a rage and ran after his wife with a sword. Luckily she was able to evade him and was wafted up to the moon by floating clouds.

After Chang Ngo left, her husband pined for her and became very ill, so one year, on the evening of the fourteenth day of the eighth moon, she sent a messenger to him who said, "Your wife has sent me to say that she knows you are lonely, but she cannot come down to earth to live with you any more. However, she will try to come to see you. Tomorrow when the moon is full, place round cakes shaped like the moon on the northwest corner of the house and call to her." The next evening the husband did as he was instructed, and he was rewarded by the visit of his wife for three evenings. And so, in honor of this legend, Chinese eat these moon cakes.

The cakes themselves are of very early origin, but the little square paper stuck in them only goes back to the Yuan dynasty, when the Chinese were tyrannized by the Mongols. Mongolian spies were quartered in private families and the Chinese were not permitted to gather into groups for conversation. No one was permitted to own a weapon—even vegetable and meat choppers were restricted to one for every ten families. Finally, according to the story, someone conceived the idea of inserting messages in the moon cakes which are universally sent to one's friends at this festival. In this way, the Chinese were able to conspire for the uprising which resulted in the overthrow of the dynasty.

✳ The Kitchen God

One superstition which is more familiar to Westerners than others is the one pertaining to the god of the kitchen. There are many special New Year deities such as the god of longevity and the god of wealth, but the kitchen god is the most famous of them all. If you have been to China and happened to glance into the kitchen, you have probably seen a picture of the kitchen god pasted on the wall near the stove.

The duty of this god is to decree the length of days of poverty or of wealth which will descend upon the family, therefore his powers are very great. He can also intercede for the family to the divine one above, so members of the household try to placate him at every turn. He notes the behavior of the members of the family and, on the twenty-third day of the twelfth moon, he reports on their conduct to the celestial Emperor. To appease the god, the family will spread a feast before the picture. Many of the dishes will be sweetmeats, so that the lips of the god will stick together so he cannot speak ill of them. At the end of the ceremony his picture will be taken down and burned with paper money, and a tiny horse will be provided to convey the god to heaven. A cricket on the hearth symbolizes the kitchen god's horse and is considered lucky because it is protected from harm. On the last day of the first moon the god returns and a new picture of him is pasted on the wall. Sacrifices will be offered to him as an act of appeasement to insure his good will throughout the year.

✳ Food Symbols

At other times of the year, the altar will display the symbols of whatever is nearest the heart of the head of the household. Pomegranates with all their seeds symbolize fertility; lotus seeds, male issue; peaches signify immortality or long life, and tangerines, good luck. Noodles are also symbols of birthdays—their length denotes longevity.

PART * II
RECIPES

Four main dishes and a soup
will serve four people.

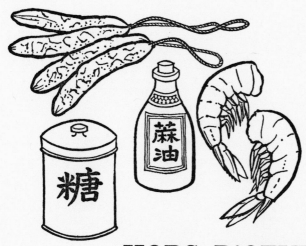

HORS D'OEUVRES

* Kidney Straws

* CH'AO YAO HUA

1 onion, chopped fine
1 tablespoon oil
1 pound pork kidneys
2 cups water

1 teaspoon sesame seed oil
1 teaspoon soy sauce
1 teaspoon lemon juice
20 rounds toast

Wash the kidney well, remove the membranes, white veins and core and soak in water for one hour, changing the water once or twice. Place in a pan with 2 cups water, bring to a boil and boil for 5 minutes. Remove from the water and drain. Heat a pan with 1 tablespoon oil and when hot, sauté the onion till it browns. Remove and drain well. Pass the kidney through a mincer and then mix with the onion. Mix the sesame seed oil, soy sauce and lemon juice, and add to the kidney. Spread on toast rounds. Serve hot.

❋ Celery

❋ CH'IN TS'AI

6 stalks tender celery
1 teaspoon soy sauce
½ teaspoon salt

½ teaspoon sugar
1 teaspoon sesame seed oil

Cut celery stalks into sections ½ inch wide and 1½ inches long. Blanch them in boiling water for 1 minute and then drain. Arrange on a serving plate and refrigerate for 1 hour. Mix other ingredients, making sure that the sugar has dissolved. Half an hour before serving, pour the sauce over the celery and allow it to marinate. Serve cold.

❋ Preserved Eggs

❋ P'I TAN

4 preserved eggs
2 tablespoons vinegar

1 tablespoon chopped ginger

Remove the lime and shell from the eggs, being careful not to break them. Wash in cold water. Cut each egg into 6 pieces lengthwise. Arrange on a dish and sprinkle with the vinegar and chopped ginger. Serve cold.

❋ Fried Shrimps

❋ CHA HSIA

12 shrimps
¼ teaspoon salt
¼ teaspoon soy sauce

½ teaspoon sherry
1 teaspoon cornstarch
enough oil for deep frying

Shell the shrimps, leaving the tails on. Devein, but be careful not to split the shrimps. Mix together the salt, soy sauce and sherry, pour over shrimps and let marinate for 10 minutes. Dip the shrimps in the cornstarch and coat well. Heat enough oil for deep-frying in a pan and lower the shrimps into this. When they are ready the shrimps will float to the top. Serve very hot on a platter.

May be served as an appetizer with cocktails.

✳ Shrimp Balls

✳ HSIA CH'IU

1 *pound shrimps*	½ *teaspoon salt*
10 *water chestnuts*	1 *egg, beaten lightly*
1 *tablespoon cornstarch*	*enough oil for deep frying*
1 *teaspoon sherry*	

Shell and devein the shrimps and mince finely. Peel the water chestnuts and mince and add to the shrimps. Mix well. Add the cornstarch, sherry, salt and egg. Mix well together and then form into balls the size of a small walnut.

Heat a pan with 2 inches of oil and when it is hot, lower the balls into it with a draining spoon; fry for about 5 minutes or until a golden brown. Serve very hot. Will make about 12 to 15 balls.

May be served on toothpicks as an appetizer.

✳ Fried Shrimps in Batter

✳ MIEN FEN CHA HSIA

1 *pound shrimps*	4 *tablespoons flour*
2 *egg whites*	*enough oil for deep frying*

Shell the shrimps but leave the tails. Devein and split the shrimps, being careful not to cut all the way through. Make a batter of the egg whites and flour. Heat the oil in a deep fryer with a wire basket. When it boils, dip the shrimps in the batter and drop one by one into the oil. When they brown and float to the top they are ready. Serve very hot.

May be served as an appetizer with cocktails.

✳ Shrimp Toast

✳ MIEN PAO HSIA

1 cup cooked shrimps, finely chopped	½ teaspoon salt
4 water chestnuts	⅛ teaspoon pepper
1 egg, slightly beaten	20 rounds of bread
1 teaspoon ground ginger	enough oil for deep frying

Peel and finely chop the water chestnuts and mix well with shrimp, egg, ginger, salt and pepper. Spread generously on rounds of bread. Heat a pan and fill up to 2 inches of oil; when it is very hot, turn down the heat and lower the shrimps on the bread into the oil and let fry for 1 to 1½ minutes or until they are golden brown. Remove from the oil and let them drain. Serve very hot.

May be served as an appetizer with cocktails.

✳ Fried Tripe

✳ CHA NIU TU

1 cow's tripe	1½ teaspoons pepper
1 teaspoon ground ginger	1 pound lard
1 teaspoon salt	

Wash the tripe thoroughly with salty cold water and cut into strips about 2½ inches long and ¾ inch wide. Dry thoroughly with paper towel. Place the lard in a thick skillet over high heat and when it is boiling add the ginger, salt and pepper. When mixed well, drop in the strips of tripe and fry till brown and curled. The number of strips will depend on the size of the tripe, but a medium-sized one will make about 40 strips.

May be served as an appetizer with cocktails.

* Cantonese Sausage

* LA CH'ANG

1 *cup rice* | ½ *pound sausage*
2 *cups water*

Wash the rice in 2 rinses of water and place in a saucepan. Add 2 scant cups of cold water and bring to a boil. Lower the heat, cover pan and simmer for about 15 minutes or until the water is all absorbed. Place the Chinese sausage on top of the rice and allow to steam for 15 minutes, until ready to serve. Slice the sausage diagonally, ⅛ inch thick, and serve hot or at room temperature on a shallow dish.

* Mushrooms Stuffed with Pork

* TUNG KU JO

Filling:
½ *pound pork, minced*
1 *tablespoon oil*
1 *teaspoon salt*
¼ *teaspoon pepper*
1 *tablespoon soy sauce*
1 *tablespoon cornstarch*
1 *stalk scallion, chopped
   fine*

12 *large mushrooms, soaked
   and stemmed*

2 *tablespoons oil*
1 *teaspoon salt*
⅛ *teaspoon pepper*
2 *tablespoons chicken stock*

Thickening:
1 *tablespoon cornstarch,*
mixed with
1 *teaspoon soy sauce*
¼ *cup water*

Mix together well the first seven ingredients. Fill the mushroom caps with this mixture. Heat a heavy pan with 2 tablespoons oil, add salt and pepper. When oil is very hot, place the mushroom caps in it with the chicken stock. Turn down the heat, cover the pan and cook slowly for 20 minutes. Remove the mushrooms and place on a flat serving plate. Mix the thickening mixture together and add to the gravy in which mushrooms were cooked. When it is thick and smooth, pour over the mushrooms and serve immediately.

✳ Roast Pork

✳ CH'A SHAO JO

1 *pound tenderloin pork*	¼ *teaspoon onion salt*
¼ *cup sherry*	¼ *teaspoon cinnamon*
½ *teaspoon salt*	¼ *cup sugar*
⅛ *teaspoon pepper*	½ *cup soy sauce*

Blend together the sherry, salt, pepper, onion salt, cinnamon, sugar and soy sauce. Pour over the meat and marinate the pork in this mixture for 2 hours, turning and basting frequently.

Preheat the oven to 350 degrees and place the meat on a rack in a baking pan and roast for 20 minutes. Turn the pork and reduce the heat to 225 degrees and roast for another 15 minutes. Cut into bite-sized pieces and serve either hot or cold.

May be served on toothpicks as an appetizer with cocktails.

✳ Barbecued Spare Ribs

✳ SHAO P'AI KU

2½ *pounds spare ribs,*	*Marinade:*
cut into 2-inch sections	1 *cup soy sauce*
	½ *cup pineapple juice*
	¼ *cup sherry*
	1½ *tablespoons brown sugar*
	1 *clove garlic, crushed*

Place the spare ribs in the marinade in a deep bowl for 6 hours; turn them frequently. Remove from the marinade and place on a broiler rack about 1 inch from medium heat and broil for about 7 minutes, basting often. Turn onto the other side and broil for another 5 minutes, and continue to baste. Serve very hot on a shallow plate.

✳ Fried Wan Tuns

✳ CHA YÜN T'UN

½ cup ground pork
¼ cup chopped shrimps
½ teaspoon salt
20 wan tun skins

1 egg, beaten
1 quart boiling water
enough oil for deep frying

Mix the pork, shrimps and salt well together and have mixture ready for filling.

Hold the wan tun skin in the left hand and place a teaspoon of filling in the center. Fold the bottom of the skin to about ¼ inch from the top. Now bend the pocket in half again, and bring the two ends to the front and seal with the beaten egg. Put on a tray and cover with a damp cloth till all the skins are made up.

Bring the water up to boiling point and slowly drop the wan tuns into this water and boil for about 5 minutes or until they rise to the top. Lift out with a perforated spoon and put in a colander. Run cold water through and drain well. Place on a plate in a single layer and let stand for about 5 hours, or until they dry.

Heat a pan with 1 inch of oil and when it is very hot, deep-fry the wan tuns till they are golden brown. Remove and drain and serve very hot.

May be served as an appetizer with cocktails.

SOUPS

✳ Beef and Turnip Soup

✳ LO PO NIU JO T'ANG

1 *pound lean beef*	3 *slices ginger*
6 *cups water*	2½ *tablespoons soy sauce*
4 *small turnips*	½ *teaspoon salt*
	⅛ *teaspoon pepper*

Cut the beef into 1-inch cubes, put in a saucepan with the water and bring to a boil. Discard the scum as it rises to the top. Lower the heat and let simmer for about 1 hour. Cut the turnips into cubes about the same size as the meat and add to the soup and simmer another 45 minutes. Add ginger, soy sauce, salt and pepper. When it comes to a boil again, serve immediately.

✷ Abalone Soup

✷ PAO YÜ T'ANG

½ pound pork
2 bamboo shoots
2 stalks celery
6 cups water

1 15-ounce can abalone
abalone liquor
½ teaspoon salt
⅛ teaspoon pepper

Slice the pork, bamboo shoots and celery all the same size and put into a saucepan with the water. Bring to a boil and let simmer for 5 minutes. Add the abalone, thinly sliced, and the abalone liquor. Season with salt and pepper, bring to a boil and simmer another 5 minutes. Serve very hot.

✷ Ham and Cabbage Soup

✷ HUO T'UI PAI TS'AI T'ANG

1 pound ham with bone
1 pound celery cabbage
8 cups water

1½ tablespoons soy sauce
½ teaspoon salt

Bring the water to a boil in a saucepan, add the ham with the bone, turn down the heat and simmer for 30 minutes. Cut the celery cabbage into quarters and into 1-inch slices. Add to the soup, and season with soy sauce and salt. Bring to a boil and simmer for another 5 minutes. Remove the ham and discard the bone. Cube the meat and return to the soup. Simmer for another 2 minutes and then serve very hot in a deep bowl.

✳ Cream of Crab Soup

4 tablespoons oil
2 slices ginger, shredded
1 stalk scallion, cut into
   1-inch sections
½ cup crab meat
½ teaspoon salt

1 tablespoon sherry
6 cups chicken broth
3 egg whites
3 tablespoons cream
3 teaspoons cornstarch

Heat a pan with the oil and when it is very hot sauté the ginger and scallion for 1 minute. Lower the heat and add the crab meat and salt; stir once or twice. Add the sherry and continue to cook for another minute. Discard the ginger. Turn the heat high and add the chicken broth, reserving ½ cup to mix with the cornstarch, and bring to a boil. Lower the heat and continue to cook. Beat the egg whites till frothy but not stiff. Blend the cream with the egg and add to the soup. Mix remaining chicken broth and cornstarch to a smooth paste and add slowly to the soup, stirring constantly. Continue to simmer for another 5 minutes and then serve very hot in a deep bowl.

✳ Egg Drop Soup

4 cups chicken stock
6 eggs
2 teaspoons soy sauce

½ teaspoon salt
1 stalk scallion, finely chopped

Heat chicken stock in a saucepan, beat eggs well and pour in a thin stream into the soup, stirring constantly. Add soy sauce, salt to taste and simmer for about 30 seconds. Serve in a deep bowl and garnish with finely chopped scallions.

✳ Fresh and Salt Pork Soup with Bamboo Shoots

✳ TUNG SUN JO T'ANG

½ pound fresh pork
¼ pound salt pork
6 cups chicken stock
2 slices ginger
2 bamboo shoots, sliced

1 tablespoon sherry
1 teaspoon salt
⅛ teaspoon pepper
1 stalk scallion, chopped fine

Cut the fresh and salt pork into slices 1 inch long and ½ inch wide. Put in a saucepan with the chicken stock. Bring to a boil and simmer for about 7 minutes. Add the ginger and bamboo shoots and simmer for 10 minutes. Add sherry, salt and pepper. Serve in a deep bowl, garnished with scallions.

✳ Lotus Stem Soup

✳ O T'ANG

1 small can lotus stem
½ pound sliced beef
6 jujubes

6 cups cold water
1 tablespoon soy sauce
½ teaspoon salt

Cut the lotus stem across into thin slices and put in a saucepan with the water, beef and jujubes. Bring to a rolling boil and let boil for about 10 seconds. Lower the heat and simmer for 45 minutes. Just before serving add the soy sauce and salt to taste. Serve very hot.

✳ Chinese Mustard Greens Soup

✳ KAI TS'AI T'ANG

½ pound lean pork
6 cups chicken broth
2 cups cut Chinese mustard
  greens

1½ teaspoons soy sauce
½ teaspoon salt

Cut pork into thin slices 1½ inches by ½ inch and put in a sauce-pan with the broth and bring to a boil. Lower the heat and simmer for about 20 minutes. Add Chinese mustard greens which have been cut into 1-inch pieces, bring to a boil again and simmer for 2 minutes. Just before serving, add the soy sauce and season to taste. Serve very hot in a deep bowl.

✳ *Watercress Soup*

✳ PI CHI T'ANG

2 *cups watercress, tightly packed*	1 *teaspoon salt*
½ *pound lean beef*	3 *cups chicken broth*
1 *tablespoon soy sauce*	3 *cups water*
1 *teaspoon oil*	¼ *teaspoon sesame seed oil*

Wash the watercress thoroughly and discard the hard stems. Dice the lean beef fine and mix well in a bowl with the soy sauce, oil and salt. Allow it to stand for about 30 minutes. Bring the chicken broth and water to a boil and add watercress. Stir well, and when it comes to the boil again add a drop of sesame seed oil and the meat. Stir thoroughly and serve very hot.

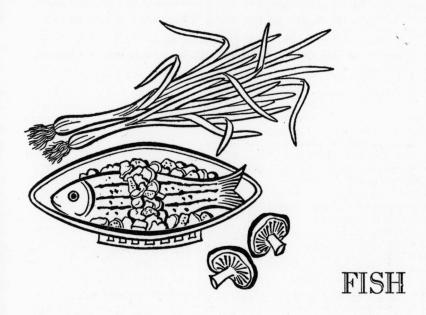

FISH

✳ Carp Sautéed with Ginger

✳ CHIANG CH'AO LI-YÜ

1 2-pound carp	4 slices ginger
2 tablespoons flour	2 stalks scallions, cut into
enough oil for deep frying	1-inch sections
4 tablespoons soy sauce	1 cup hot water
2 tablespoons sherry	1 teaspoon salt
½ teaspoon sugar	

Clean the fish but do not remove the head and tail. Score the sides about 1 inch deep, and rub the fish on both sides with the flour. Heat a pan and fill up to 1½ inches of oil. When oil is very hot, lower the fish into it and fry for 1 minute on each side. Turn down the heat and continue to fry 2 minutes on one side and

1 minute on the other. Remove the fish and pour off the oil. Return the fish to the oily pan and add the soy sauce, sherry, sugar, ginger, scallions, salt and water. Cover the pan and turn up the heat and cook quickly for 8 minutes. Serve very hot in a shallow bowl.

✳ Sweet and Sour Carp

✳ T'ANG TS'U LI-YÜ

1 2-pound carp	Sauce:
2 tablespoons cornstarch	2 tablespoons oil
2 tablespoons water	¼ cup soy sauce
4 tablespoons oil for fish	½ cup honey
2 tablespoons oil for vegetables	1 cup vinegar
1 small onion, sliced	1 tablespoon cornstarch
1 carrot, diced	
1 white turnip, diced	

Clean and scale the fish, but do not remove the head and tail. Drain and dry it well. Make diagonal slashes 1 inch apart down the sides of the fish. Mix the cornstarch with the water and coat the fish well with it.

Heat a pan with 4 tablespoons oil and hold the fish over the pan by the head, basting the fish with the hot oil until the exposed flesh and the skin become brown and crisp. Drain the fish on a paper towel and then arrange on a serving platter.

Reheat the pan with 2 tablespoons of oil and sauté the onion, carrot and turnip for 1 minute. Stir in the sauce mixture and bring it to a boil. Simmer for 2 minutes or until it becomes thick and smooth. Pour the sauce and vegetables over the fish and serve at once.

✳ Red-Cooked Flounder

1 2-pound flounder
6 tablespoons oil
1 slice ginger
1 stalk scallion, cut into
    1-inch sections
1 clove garlic
6 mushrooms, soaked and
    sliced
½ bamboo shoot, sliced

1 teaspoon salt
7 teaspoons soy sauce
2 teaspoons sherry
¼ pound fat pork, cut into
    small slices
1 cup chicken stock
½ teaspoon sugar
1 clove anise

Wash the fish but do not remove the head and tail. Score the sides about 1½ inches apart and 1 inch deep. Heat a pan with the oil and when it is hot, sauté the fish for 3 minutes on one side and 2 minutes on the other. Add the ginger, scallion, garlic, mushrooms, bamboo shoots, salt, soy sauce, sherry and fat pork, and slowly the stock. Turn the heat high; add sugar and anise. When the liquid starts to boil, turn the heat low and cover. Simmer for 20 minutes and serve very hot in a shallow bowl.

✳ Sweet-Sour Sea Bass

1 2-pound bass
1 teaspoon salt
⅛ teaspoon pepper
1 tablespoon soy sauce
enough oil for deep frying
1 green pepper, diced

Sauce:
¾ cup vinegar
¼ cup sherry
2 teaspoons sugar
3 tablespoons soy sauce
1 teaspoon cornstarch
1 cup water

Clean fish and do not remove the head and tail. Score the sides about 1½ inches apart and 1 inch deep. Season with pepper, salt, and soy sauce. Allow it to stand for 10 minutes to absorb the flavor.

Mix the ingredients for the sauce, making sure to blend the cornstarch well. Place in a pan, bring to a boil. Add the green pepper and simmer for 10 minutes. Set it aside and keep it very hot.

Heat another pan filled up to 2 inches of oil and when it is very hot lower the fish in slowly and fry one side for 5 minutes and 2 minutes on the other. Arrange on a hot platter and pour the hot sauce over it and serve immediately.

❊ Steamed Sea Bass

❊CHEN LU-YÜ

1 2-pound sea bass	1¼ tablespoons fermented
1 tablespoon oil	black bean, mashed
¾ teaspoon salt	2 stalks scallions, cut into
1 teaspoon sugar	1-inch sections
1½ teaspoons sherry	2 slices ginger

Clean the fish and do not remove the head and tail. Score both sides of the fish with diagonal slashes about 1½ inches apart. Drain the fish and dry it well. Rub the inside and outside of the fish with the oil, making sure that the gashes are well coated. Heat an ovenproof serving bowl and place a rack in a pan filled to 2 inches of boiling water. Place the fish in the serving bowl and sprinkle with salt, sugar and sherry, and cover with the black beans, scallions and ginger. Place the bowl on the rack, cover and turn up the heat. Steam for 15 minutes and serve very hot in the shallow bowl.

✻ Braised Lake Trout

✻ HUNG SHAO TSUN-YÜ

1 3-pound trout	2 stalks scallions, cut into
2 teaspoons salt	½-inch sections
4 teaspoons oil	1 ounce ham, cut into shreds
3 tablespoons soy sauce	½ cup hot water
4 slices ginger	2 teaspoons sugar
	2 tablespoons sherry

Clean the fish and do not remove the head and tail. Set it aside to drain. When it is dry, rub both inside and out with salt. Heat a pan with the oil and when it is very hot, sauté the fish on one side for about 3 minutes, and the other side for 2 minutes, basting continually. Do not turn again. Pour the soy sauce evenly over the fish, and then add the ginger, scallions and ham. Pour the water in the pan slowly and bring the sauce to a boil. Braise for 2 or 3 minutes. Add sugar and sherry and bring to the boil again. Turn the heat low and simmer for 15 minutes and serve very hot on a shallow platter.

✻ Steamed Fish with Mushrooms

✻ TUNG KU CHEN YÜ

1½ pounds porgy	⅛ teaspoon monosodium
8 dried mushrooms	glutamate
⅛ pound Smithfield ham,	1 teaspoon salt
shredded	¾ teaspoon sugar
3 slices ginger, finely chopped	⅛ teaspoon pepper
1 stalk scallion, sliced fine	3 tablespoons oil
2 teaspoons soy sauce	

Wash and soak the mushrooms in hot water and when soft, stem and cut them into ¼-inch strips. Cut the ham into shreds.

Wash the fish and dry it well. Rub the inside and outside with the oil. Place on a hot shallow dish and cover the fish with the mushrooms, ham, ginger, scallion, soy sauce, seasonings and the remainder of the oil. Place a rack in a pan filled up to 2 inches of water. When the water is boiling furiously, place the fish on the rack and steam for 15 minutes. Remove from the steamer and serve very hot.

✳ Steamed Sole in Savory Custard

✳ CHI TAN CHEN PAN-YÜ

2 pounds filet of sole	¼ green pepper, chopped fine
1 tablespoon oil	4 eggs
1 tablespoon cornstarch	1 cup chicken stock
1½ tablespoons soy sauce	1 teaspoon salt
2 stalks scallions, chopped fine	

Cut the filet into 1-inch sections and place in a shallow bowl. Blend the oil, cornstarch and soy sauce and sprinkle over the fish. Add the scallion and the green pepper. Beat the eggs well and add to the stock with the salt. Mix well and pour over the fish. Place a rack in a pan and fill up to 2 inches of water. Place the bowl on the rack and cover the pan. Steam for 1 hour. Serve very hot.

✳ Sole Sautéed in Egg

✳ CHI TAN CH'AO PAN-YÜ

1½ pounds filet of sole	2 stalks scallions, chopped fine
3 eggs	
1 teaspoon salt	2 slices ginger, chopped fine
2 tablespoons cornstarch	1 tablespoon sherry
4 tablespoons oil	2 tablespoons water

Cut the fish into pieces about 1½ inches long. Beat the eggs lightly and add half the salt. Slowly fold in the cornstarch and mix together till it is smooth. Dip the fish pieces in this mixture till they are well covered. Heat a pan with the oil, and when it is very hot sauté the fish for 2 minutes on one side and 1 minute on the other.

To the remaining egg mixture add the salt, scallion, ginger, sherry and water. Blend well and add to the fish and cook for about 2 minutes or until the sauce thickens, stirring constantly and turning the fish two or three times during this process.

Serve very hot on a shallow platter.

✳ Pike Sautéed with Chinese Vegetables

✳ CH'ING TS'AI CH'AO SO-TZU-YÜ

1 *pound filet of pike*	3 *water chestnuts*
1 *tablespoon cornstarch*	12 *snow peas*
1 *teaspoon sherry*	¼ *cup water*
¾ *teaspoon salt*	⅛ *teaspoon monosodium*
2 *tablespoons oil*	*glutamate*
1 *clove garlic*	¼ *teaspoon sugar*
¼ *pound celery cabbage*	⅓ *teaspoon pepper*
2 *slices bamboo shoots*	8 *slices ginger*

Cut the bamboo shoots into shreds. Peel the water chestnuts and slice them. Shred the celery cabbage and stem the snow peas, but leave the pods intact.

Cut the fish diagonally into very thin slices. Mix the cornstarch with the sherry and ¼ teaspoon of salt and when well mixed, marinate fish in the mixture. Heat pan with 1 tablespoon of oil and ¼ teaspoon of salt, and when it is very hot add the garlic and brown it. Sauté the cabbage, the bamboo shoot slices, water chestnuts and snow peas for 1 minute. Add the water, monosodium glutamate, sugar and pepper, cover and continue to cook for 2 minutes. Remove the vegetables and set aside. Wipe the pan and heat again and add the remaining oil, salt and ginger. Add the fish and sauté for ½ minute, stirring constantly, being careful not to break the fish. Add the vegetables and sauté for 1 minute more. Serve very hot.

✳ Fish Fried in Batter

✳ MIEN FEN CHA YÜ

½ pound filet of fish	¼ teaspoon salt
1 cup flour	⅛ teaspoon pepper
2 teaspoons baking powder	enough oil for deep frying
¾ cup water, scant	

Sift the baking powder with the flour and mix with water to make a thin batter. Do not have it too runny. Set it aside for a few minutes.

Cut the filet of fish into 1-inch strips; season with pepper and salt.

Heat a pan filled up to 2 inches of oil and bring it to boiling point. Dip the fish in the batter and drop it in the oil and fry till it is golden brown. Serve immediately with side dishes of thick, imported soy sauce.

SEA FOOD

✳ Sautéed Abalone with Oyster Sauce

✳ HAO YU CH'AO PAO YÜ

1 15-ounce can abalone
1 cup lean pork
½ cup mushrooms
¼ cup water chestnuts
2 bamboo shoots
2 teaspoons oyster sauce
1 slice ginger, chopped
1 teaspoon sherry
½ teaspoon sesame seed oil
½ cup water
1 tablespoon oil

½ teaspoon salt
1 clove garlic
½ cup liquor from abalone

Thickening:
1 tablespoon cornstarch
mixed with
1 teaspoon sugar
1 teaspoon soy sauce
1 tablespoon water

65

Cut the abalone into 1-inch cubes and chop up fine the pork, mushrooms, water chestnuts and bamboo shoots. Mix well together the oyster sauce, ginger, sherry, sesame seed oil and the water.

Heat pan with the oil, salt and garlic and when it is very hot add the abalone and the pork and sauté for 1 minute. Add the mushrooms, water chestnuts and bamboo shoots and continue to sauté for 1 minute more. Add the seasoning mixture and stir once and slowly add the abalone liquor. Cover, bring to a boil and simmer for 1 minute. Add the thickening and bring to a boil, stirring constantly. When the liquid is thick and smooth, remove immediately and serve.

✳ Braised Eels

✳ HUNG SHAO SHAN YÜ

1 *pound eels*	2 *tablespoons sherry*
1 *teaspoon salt*	1 *cup water*
⅛ *teaspoon pepper*	
2 *tablespoons oil*	*Marinade:*
½ *clove garlic*	1 *tablespoon cornstarch*
4 *slices ginger*	1 *tablespoon soy sauce*
2 *onions, sliced*	4 *tablespoons water*
8 *mushrooms, soaked and*	
sliced	

Cut the eels into 2-inch lengths and rub with salt and pepper. Heat a pan with the oil and sauté the garlic for 1 minute and discard. Sauté the eels in the pan till they are brown. Transfer them into a saucepan and add ginger, onions, mushrooms, sherry and water. Bring to a boil, cover and simmer for 10 minutes. Mix the ingredients for the marinade and add to the liquid and simmer for 5 minutes more. Stir once or twice and season with pepper and salt to taste. Serve hot in a shallow bowl.

✳ Stuffed Clams

✳ JO SUNG KO-LI

2½ pounds clams with shells
¼ pound minced pork
1 slice ginger, chopped fine
1 stalk scallion, chopped fine
3 teaspoons sherry

½ teaspoon salt
½ teaspoon sugar
1 teaspoon soy sauce
¼ cup chicken stock
2 tablespoons oil

Wash the clams well in cold water and then pour boiling water over them to open. Remove the clams from the shells and try to preserve the liquid. Mince the clams and mix with the meat and the clam juice. Add the ginger, scallion, sherry, salt, sugar and soy sauce and mix well. Fill the shells with this mixture and arrange on a baking dish containing the chicken stock and oil. Preheat the oven to 450 degrees and bake for about 10 minutes, or until the pork is no longer pink. Serve very hot in the baking dish.

✳ Crab Meat with Eggs

✳ HSIEH JO CHI TAN

1 cup crab meat
2 tablespoons oil
1 onion, shredded
4 eggs, lightly beaten

1 teaspoon salt
⅛ teaspoon pepper
1 stalk scallion, cut into
    1-inch sections

Remove broken shells and cartilage from the crab meat and flake. Heat a pan with the oil and when it is very hot add the onion and sauté till the shreds are transparent. Add the crab meat and sauté for 2 or 3 minutes, stirring occasionally. Add the eggs and continue to stir. When mixture resembles a light custard, remove from the heat and turn onto a hot plate. Sprinkle the scallion over the egg and serve immediately.

❋ Crabs with Steamed Rice

❋ HSIEH FAN

2 cups glutinous rice
4 cups water

Marinade:
¼ cup sherry
2 tablespoons soy sauce
1 slice ginger, finely chopped
2 stalks scallions, finely
    chopped

4 large hard-shelled crabs
1 tablespoon soy sauce
1 tablespoon oil
½ teaspoon salt
½ teaspoon sugar

Bring the rice to a boil with the water, turn down the heat and simmer for about 30 minutes or until the water is absorbed. Set aside. Marinate the crabs in the sherry mixture for 30 minutes, turning them occasionally. Season the rice with the 1 tablespoon soy sauce, oil, sugar and salt and put it in a deep, heatproof serving bowl. Arrange the crabs on the rice and pour the marinade over all. Put the dish on a rack in a steaming vessel, being careful that the water does not overflow into the bowl, and steam for 1½ hours. Serve very hot in the bowl.

❋ Sautéed Frogs' Legs

❋ CH'AO T'IEN-CHI

1 pound frogs' legs
6 mushrooms
6 water chestnuts
4 tablespoons oil
1 clove garlic
3 slices ginger
2 stalks scallions, chopped fine
1 tablespoon sherry

1 small green pepper

Thickening:
⅓ cup chicken stock
mixed with
1 teaspoon sugar
1 teaspoon cornstarch
2 tablespoons water

Soak the mushrooms in half a cup of hot water for 30 minutes, stem and slice them thin. Peel the water chestnuts and slice thin. Cut the frogs' legs into two.

Heat a pan with the oil and when it is very hot add the garlic and ginger and stir once. Add the frogs' legs and sauté for 2 minutes, stirring constantly. Add the scallions and sherry and continue to cook for another 2 minutes. Discard the garlic and ginger and remove the frogs' legs and keep warm. Cut the green pepper into 1-inch squares, and add to the hot pan. Add the mushrooms and water chestnuts, and sauté together for 2 minutes. Remove the vegetables. Add thickening to the hot oil, and cook over medium heat till it is thick. Add the frogs' legs and vegetables and cook for 2 minutes, stirring constantly. Serve immediately.

✳ Lobster Sautéed with Vegetables

✳ CH'ING TS'AI CH'AO LUNG HSIA

1 *pound cooked lobster, diced*	*Seasoning:*
6 *dried mushrooms*	1 *teaspoon soy sauce*
4 *water chestnuts*	*mixed with*
½ *cup peas*	2 *tablespoons sherry*
1 *tablespoon oil*	1 *slice ginger, shredded*
1 *teaspoon salt*	1 *tablespoon mushroom liquid*
1 *clove garlic, crushed*	
8 *fresh mushrooms, diced*	*Thickening:*
½ *cup diced celery*	1 *tablespoon cornstarch*
½ *cup diced Chinese cabbage*	*mixed with*
½ *cup diced onion*	½ *cup water*
½ *cup diced bamboo shoots*	¼ *teaspoon pepper*
½ *cup chicken stock*	1 *teaspoon sugar*
¼ *cup roasted almonds,*	1 *tablespoon soy sauce*
crushed	

Soak the dried mushrooms in ½ cup water for 30 minutes; stem and dice them. Peel the water chestnuts and dice them. Boil the peas and keep them hot for garnishing. Heat pan with the oil, salt and garlic. When it is very hot, add the dried and fresh mushrooms, celery, cabbage, onion, bamboo shoots and water chestnuts and sauté them for about 1 minute, stirring constantly. Add the lobster and cook for another minute, and then add the seasoning. When it comes to a boil, add the chicken stock. Cover the pan and when it comes to a boil again, simmer for 1 minute and then add the thickening, stirring constantly. When it is very hot and thick, serve in a shallow bowl and garnish with almonds and peas.

✳ Lobster Cantonese

✳ CH'AO LUNG HSIA

2 1-pound lobsters
½ pound lean pork
4 stalks scallions, minced fine
1½ teaspoons salt
1 teaspoon pepper
4 tablespoons oil
1 stalk celery, finely sliced
1 cup chicken stock
2 eggs

Thickening:
2½ tablespoons flour
mixed with
2 teaspoons soy sauce
¼ cup lobster liquid (add water to make up the amount if not enough)

Split the raw lobsters in half lengthwise and pick off the broken shells. Cut off the legs and claws with poultry shears. Discard the very small legs and wash the large legs and claws. Cut them at the joints with shears and crack them well enough with a nutcracker so that the meat can be extracted easily. Cut the lobster in the shells into 1½-inch sections. Put all in a large bowl and save the lobster juice. Mince pork and add the scallions, ½ teaspoon salt and the pepper.

Heat pan with the oil and the remaining 1 teaspoon salt and when it is very hot sauté the pork and celery for 1 minute. Add the lobster and claws and sauté for ½ minute and then slowly add the chicken stock and bring to a boil. Cover the pan, reduce the heat and cook for 10 minutes, turning the lobster once. Add the thickening to the pan and simmer for 4 minutes. Beat the eggs well and pour over the lobster. After 1 minute, turn off the heat and pour into a large hot bowl and serve immediately.

✻ Oysters Fried in Batter

✻ MIEN FEN CHA LI HUANG

1 cup flour	¼ teaspoon salt
2 teaspoons baking powder	⅛ teaspoon pepper
¾ cup water (scant)	enough oil for deep frying
1 cup small oysters	

Sift the baking powder with the flour and mix with the water to make a thin batter. Set it aside for a few minutes. Season the oysters with pepper and salt. Heat a pan filled to 2 inches of oil and bring it to a boil. Dip the oysters in the batter and drop into the oil and fry till golden brown. Serve immediately with side dishes of thick, imported soy sauce.

✻ Oyster Patties

✻ LI HUANG PING

4 eggs, beaten	¼ cup oyster liquid
4 stalks scallions	⅛ teaspoon pepper
1½ cups small oysters	1 teaspoon salt
4 tablespoons flour	2 tablespoons oil
½ teaspoon baking powder	

Cut the scallions into ½-inch sections and add to the well-beaten eggs. Pour the oysters into this mixture and stir well together. Sift the baking powder with the flour and make it into a smooth paste with the oyster liquid. Season with pepper and salt and add to the egg mixture. Heat a pan and grease it with a drop of oil. Spoon enough of the oyster mixture to make patties 2 inches in diameter. Sauté for 1 minute on one side or until the pancake sets, turn onto the other side and sauté till brown. Serve very hot.

✳ Shrimps Fried in Shells

✳ CHA HSIA LU

1½ pounds large shrimps
enough oil for deep frying

Marinade:
1 teaspoon sugar
4 tablespoons soy sauce
2 tablespoons sherry
1 teaspoon chopped ginger
1 stalk scallion, chopped fine

Clean the shrimps, remove the legs and the veins. The black vein in the back may be removed by pulling it from the head end. If unsuccessful, use a knife and break the shell but leave the shell on. Dry the shrimps well.

Heat a pan filled up to 2 inches of oil and when it is very hot, lower the shrimps into it and fry for about 5 minutes or until they turn red. Remove to a shallow bowl. Mix the marinade together, pour over the shrimps and let them marinate for ½ hour or until you are ready to serve. Serve cold.

✳ Shrimps Sautéed with Bamboo Shoots

✳ TUNG SUN CH'AO HSIA

1½ pounds shrimps
3 slices ginger
2 bamboo shoots
2 tablespoons cornstarch
1 teaspoon salt

2 tablespoons sherry
1 stalk scallion, cut into
½-inch sections
3 tablespoons oil

Cut the ginger into ½-inch pieces and the bamboo shoots into ½-inch cubes. Shell and devein the shrimps and cut into ½-inch pieces. Mix with the cornstarch, salt, sherry, scallions and ginger.

Heat pan with the oil, and when it is very hot add the shrimp mixture. Stir once, and then add the bamboo shoots and sauté together for about 4 minutes. Serve very hot on a shallow plate.

✱ Sautéed Shrimps with Peas

✱ CH'ING TOU CH'AO HSIA

1 pound shrimps	Thickening:
2 tablespoons oil	2 tablespoons cornstarch
¼ pound peas	mixed with
½ cup chicken stock	2 teaspoons soy sauce
	¼ cup water

Shell and devein the shrimps and cut them into ½-inch pieces. Heat a pan with the oil and when it is very hot sauté the shrimps for about 2 minutes, stirring constantly. Add the peas and the chicken stock slowly. Cover the pan, turn down the heat and simmer for 2 minutes. Pour the thickening over the shrimps and cook for 1 or 2 minutes more or until the sauce is thick and clear. Serve very hot.

✱ Phoenix-Tail Shrimps

✱ FENG WEI HSIA

1 pound medium-sized shrimps	1 teaspoon salt
1 egg	enough oil for deep frying
4 tablespoons water	Pepper-and- salt mix
4 tablespoons flour	

Shell the shrimps but keep the tails on. Devein but be careful not to split them in two. Beat egg, mix with flour, water and salt.

Heat a pan filled up to 1 inch of oil. Dip each shrimp by the tail in the flour mixture and lower slowly into the boiling oil. Fry on one side for 1½ minutes and the other for another minute. Remove from oil and drain for a few seconds on absorbent paper and serve immediately with side dishes of pepper-and-salt mix.

DUCK

✳ Peking Duck

✳ PEICHING K'AO YA

1 6-pound duck
enough pepper and salt
   to rub into duck
5 slices ginger
1 onion sliced
2 tablespoons oil
enough vegetable paste to rub
   into duck and for table
   condiment

10 stalks scallions, cut into
   2-inch sections

Pancakes or Pao Ping:
2½ cups flour
1 cup boiling water
1 teaspoon salt
1½ tablespoons oil

Pancakes: Sift salt with the flour in a large bowl, add the water slowly into the flour, and mix thoroughly. Remove the dough to a floured board and knead well. Pull the dough into a long rope and cut into 24 pieces. Pat each piece out on the palm of the hand till it is about 2 inches in diameter, and then roll it out as thin as possible with a rolling pin, to look like a pancake. Oil both sides of the pancakes and dust with flour. Heat a pan, cook the pancakes over low heat, covered, for 1½ minutes on each side till they brown. Fold, place on a hot plate, and pile one on top of another and cover with a damp cloth to keep them fresh.

Duck: Clean the duck well, being careful to get rid of all the hairs. Cut off the tail and the oil sacs and discard. Dry the duck carefully and when it is very dry, rub the breast and back with salt and pepper. Put the 5 slices of ginger and the onion in the duck. Preheat the oven to 250 degrees and when it is hot put 2 tablespoons of the oil and the duck into the roasting pan and roast for 2 hours. Remove from the oven and rub the vegetable paste over the back, breast and legs. Return to the oven, breast downward, for 30 minutes. Remove from the heat and coat the skin again with the paste, and then return it to the oven breast upward for another 20 minutes. By this time the skin should be very crisp.

Cut the pieces of skin about 2 inches square with as little of the meat as possible, and serve on a platter. Place pancakes on the table and the scallions and vegetable paste on side dishes. Let the guests make their own sandwiches of pancakes with a filling of crisp duck skin and scallions.

The rest of the duck is generally reserved for another meal.

✳ *Szechuan Duck*

✳ CHU'AN YA

1 *5-pound duck*
4 *stalks scallions, cut into*
    2½-inch sections
4 *slices ginger*
1 *clove anise*

3 *tablespoons sherry*
5 *tablespoons soy sauce*
2 *teaspoons sugar*
1 *cup cold water*
vegetable paste

Trim the duck, cut off the tail and oil sacs, tuck the wings under the body and place in a large skillet. Put half the scallions and 2 slices of ginger inside the duck and the rest in the skillet. Break the anise and sprinkle it and the sugar on the duck. Pour the sherry, soy sauce and water over it. Cover the skillet, turn the heat high and bring the liquid to a boil. Lower the heat and simmer for 1½ hours, turning the duck two or three times during this process, being careful not to puncture the skin. Remove it, drain and place in the refrigerator for five hours to dry thoroughly. Correct seasoning in the gravy by adding sugar, salt and soy sauce. Set the gravy aside.

Three quarters of an hour before serving, preheat the oven to 500 degrees. Place the duck, breast downward, on a rack and roast for 15 minutes. Turn the duck, increase the heat to the highest point and roast for another 10 minutes or until the skin is brown and crisp. Carve the duck so that each slice will have a piece of skin on it. Serve on a flat plate with Chinese steamed bread as accompaniment and make a sandwich of them. Heat the gravy and serve in a gravy boat. Serve with vegetable paste on side dishes as a table condiment.

✻ Roast Duck

✻ K'AO YA

1 3-pound duck	1 clove garlic
½ large saucepan water	2 slices ginger
5 teaspoons soy sauce	3 cloves anise
5 teaspoons salt	enough oil for deep frying
1 stalk scallion	pepper-and-salt mix

Wash the duck well and cut off the tail and oil sacs and discard. Put in a large saucepan and cover with cold water. Add the soy sauce, salt, scallion, garlic, ginger and the anise. Bring the water to a boil and then turn down the heat and simmer for 1½ hours. Remove the duck carefully; let it drain and cool.

Heat a deep pan and fill up to 2 or 3 inches of oil. When it is very hot, lower the duck into the oil and fry it for about 6 minutes, turning once or twice and basting continually till it is golden brown. Chop into small pieces, Chinese style, and arrange on a dish, skin side upward. Serve very hot with pepper-and-salt mix.

✳ Spiced Duck

✳ WU HSIANG YA

1 5-pound duck	2 teaspoons powdered five spices
¾ cup sherry	enough water to half-cover duck
¾ cup soy sauce	

Clean the duck well and remove all the hairs. Cut off the tail and oil sacs and discard. Place in a large pan and pour the sherry and soy sauce over it. Bring to a boil over high heat and brown each side of the duck for 2 minutes. Coat the duck well on each side with the powdered spice and add enough water to half-cover the duck. Bring to a boil, cover, lower the heat and simmer for 1½ hours, turning every twenty minutes. Chop it up Chinese style or carve in the Western way.

Serve either hot or cold.

✳ West Lake Steamed Duck

✳ HSI HU YA

1 5-pound duck	1 clove anise
3½ teaspoons soy sauce	4 slices ginger
enough oil for deep frying	1 tablespoon sherry

1 teaspoon honey
1 tablespoon salt
enough water to cover duck
½ cup shredded bamboo
    shoots
6 mushrooms, soaked and
    shredded
½ cup sliced celery

Thickening:
  1 tablespoon cornstarch
mixed with
  ½ cup water

½ cup shredded Smithfield
    ham
½ cup Chinese parsley

Cut off the tail and oil sacs of the duck, wash well and dry thoroughly. Rub the duck with half the soy sauce. Heat a deep frying pan with the oil and when it is very hot, fry the duck for about 5 minutes or until it becomes golden brown. Remove from the oil and rinse in a large pan of cold water. Place the duck in a deep bowl, sprinkle the rest of the soy sauce, anise, ginger, sherry, honey and salt on it. Add enough water to cover the duck. Place a rack in a large pan and fill up to 2 inches of furiously boiling water. Place the bowl on the rack, cover tightly and steam over medium heat for 1½ hours. Be sure that the steaming water does not dry up. When adding water be sure that it is boiling.

Remove the duck and cool. Remove the bones, but be careful not to break the skin. Strain the liquid and set the sauce aside. Place the duck in a deep bowl with the skin on top and steam for another 15 minutes. Remove from the steamer, but keep hot. Heat the gravy in a pan and add the bamboo, mushrooms and celery and simmer slowly for 10 minutes. Add the thickening gradually till the sauce becomes thick and smooth. Pour the sauce over the duck and sprinkle the ham on top. Garnish with parsley.

✳ Steamed Duck

✳ CHEN YA

1 5-pound duck
2 pounds celery cabbage
    cut into 1-inch sections
4 ounces sliced Smithfield ham

1 teaspoon salt
1 tablespoon lotus seeds
6 tablespoons oil

Wash the duck well and pull off the hairs with a tweezer. Cut off and discard the tail and oil sacs. Mix half of the cabbage with the ham, salt and lotus seeds and stuff the duck with it. Sew up the openings securely.

Heat a large pan with the oil. When it is very hot, brown the duck in it for about 15 minutes. Line the remainder of the cabbage in a large serving basin, and place the duck on top of the cabbage. Have the water in the steamer boiling furiously, place the basin in it and cover with a tight lid. Steam the duck for about 3 hours or until it is tender. Serve very hot in the basin.

✳ Red-Cooked Duck

✳ HUNG SHAO YA

1 3-pound duck
2 slices ginger
1 stalk scallion
5 mushrooms, soaked
2 teaspoons sesame seed oil

3 teaspoons salt
3 teaspoons sherry
3 teaspoons soy sauce
2 teaspoons sugar
half a saucepan water

Wash the duck and remove the tail and oil sacs and discard. Place the duck in a saucepan with enough water to cover. Add the rest of the ingredients and bring to a boil. Turn down the heat and simmer for 1½ hours. Serve in a deep bowl with the gravy.

✳ Eight Precious Duck

✳ PA PAO YA

1 6-pound duck
½ cup barley
8 mushrooms, soaked and diced

¼ cup lotus seeds
¼ cup shelled and blanched
    chestnuts

½ cup diced pork
¼ cup shelled and blanched
    almonds
1 teaspoon salt
2 teaspoons sherry
2 tablespoons soy sauce

1 teaspoon sugar
2 cups stock
4 tablespoons soy sauce for gravy
4 stalks scallions
4 slices ginger
1 teaspoon sugar for the gravy

Boil the barley for about 20 minutes or until it is soft. Pour away the hot water and soak barley in cold water till required. Remove the green centers from the lotus seeds as they are bitter. Drain the barley and mix with mushrooms, lotus seeds, chestnuts, pork, almonds, salt, sherry, 2 tablespoons soy sauce and 1 teaspoon sugar. Mix thoroughly, stuff in the duck and sew up the opening.

Place the duck in a deep saucepan and add the stock with 4 tablespoons soy sauce, scallions, ginger and 1 teaspoon sugar. Bring the liquid to a boil and then turn down the heat and simmer for 1 hour, turning the duck twice in the process. Place the duck carefully in a large bowl and pour the gravy over it. Serve very hot.

✳ Heavenly Boiled Duck

✳ SHEN HSIEN YA

1 6-pound duck
1 onion, minced
1 teaspoon bean paste

2 quarts dry white wine
2 teaspoons salt

Wash the duck, cut off the tail and oil sacs and discard them. Dry the duck thoroughly. Place the onions and bean paste inside the duck. Place the wine in a large saucepan and bring to a boil. Add the salt and lower the duck into the liquid. Cover the saucepan tightly and place on an asbestos pad over low heat and simmer for 5 hours. Remove very carefully onto a deep serving bowl, cover with broth and serve immediately.

* Jade Belt Duck

1 4-pound duck	2 tablespoons sherry
4 cups water	3 tablespoons soy sauce
1 pound Smithfield ham, sliced thin	½ teaspoon salt
2 bunches leeks	4 slices ginger, chopped fine

Clean the duck well, cut off the tail and oil sacs and discard. Put the duck in a saucepan with about 4 cups water or enough to cover it. Bring to a boil and simmer for 15 minutes. Remove the duck and reserve the broth. Bone the duck and cut the meat into slices 2 inches by 1 inch. Wrap the ham around the meat and tie with the leek leaves; arrange attractively in a deep ovenproof bowl. Add sherry, soy sauce, salt, ginger and the broth. Place the bowl on a rack in a large saucepan filled up to 2 inches of boiling water and steam for about 1 hour. Serve in the hot bowl.

* Duck with Chestnuts

1 6-pound duck	1 onion, quartered
1 pound pork, cut into 1-inch cubes	½ pound small chestnuts, shelled and blanched
½ pound mushrooms, soaked and stemmed	6 slices ginger
enough water to cover duck	1 cup soy sauce

Chop the duck into 2-inch pieces; wash and dry them carefully. Place pieces in a saucepan with the pork, mushrooms, onions, ginger and chestnuts. Add the soy sauce and enough water to barely cover the ingredients. Bring to a boil and turn down the heat to its lowest point and cover the saucepan tightly. Simmer for about 2 hours. Serve the duck, pork and chestnuts in a shallow bowl and pour enough sauce to only half-cover the duck.

✳ Wild Duck

✳ CH'AO YEH YA

1 3-pound wild duck
½ cup oil
 1 onion, chopped
 1 teaspoon bean sauce
    (Hoisin sauce)
½ clove anise
¼ cup sherry

1 cup stock
½ cup soy sauce
½ cup bean curd
½ teaspoon salt
 1 teaspoon sugar
 1 teaspoon sesame seed oil

Chop the duck up in the Chinese manner, through the backbone and then into pieces about 1 inch square. Heat a deep pan with the oil, and when it is very hot add the duck and sauté slowly over low heat. Add the onion, bean sauce and anise, and continue to sauté, stirring constantly for 15 minutes. Add the sherry and cover. Lower the heat and simmer for 30 minutes. Add stock, soy sauce, bean curd and salt. Bring to a boil and then add the sugar and oil. Stir once or twice and when it reaches boiling point, remove from the fire and serve immediately in a bowl.

CHICKEN

✳ Roast Chicken

✳ SHAO CHI

1 3-pound chicken
3 stalks scallions, cut into
   1-inch sections
½ cup sherry
1 teaspoon sugar

2 pieces ginger, sliced
1 cup soy sauce
1 teaspoon salt
3 cups water

Mix all the ingredients, except the chicken, place in a large saucepan and bring to a boil. Add chicken, turn up the heat and when it comes to a boil again lower the heat, cover and simmer for 15 minutes. Turn off the heat and let the chicken stand in the liquid for another 15 minutes, turning once again.

Remove the chicken from the liquid and allow it to drain. Transfer to a roasting pan. Preheat the oven to 450 degrees and place the chicken on a lower rack and roast for 30 minutes. The chicken should be brown and crisp.

Cut the chicken in half through the backbone. Remove the legs and wings and cut into three pieces. Cut the halves of the chicken into 5 or 6 pieces and then arrange on a serving dish skin side upward. Serve with side dishes of pepper-and-salt mix.

✳ Boiled White Chicken

✳ PAI CHU CHI

1 3-pound chicken
2 stalks scallions

3 thick slices ginger
enough water to cover chicken

Place the chicken in a large saucepan and cover with water. Add scallions and ginger and cover. Bring the water to a boil, turn off the heat and let the chicken stand in the hot water for an hour. Remove from the water and allow it to drain for about 15 minutes and put in the refrigerator before it has cooled. When cold, cut the chicken up Chinese style and serve with side dishes of thick soy sauce.

✳ Salted Chicken

✳ HSIEN CHI

1 2½-pound chicken
2 pounds kitchen salt

Wash the chicken and dry it well with a cloth. Hang it in a draft to dry thoroughly. Put the salt in a good-sized heavy pot and cook it over medium heat. When the salt is very hot, remove the pot from the heat and remove half the salt. Make a hole in the center of the remaining salt, but do not expose the bottom of the pan. Place the chicken, neck downward, in the salt and pack the remainder of the salt around the chicken. Cover the pan and cook over very low heat for about 1 hour. Remove the chicken from the salt, chop it Chinese style and serve immediately. This may also be served cold.

✳ Drunken Chicken

✳ TSUI CHI

1 2-pound spring chicken	1 teaspoon salt
3 quarts water	enough sherry to cover chicken

Wash the chicken well and truss tightly. Bring the water in a large saucepan to a rolling boil and add the salt. While the water is still bubbling, lower the chicken into it, and tightly cover the saucepan. Remove it from the heat, place in a cool place and allow it to stand till the water is cooled. Transfer the chicken into a large jar and cover completely with sherry. Seal tightly. Place it in the coolest part of the refrigerator for about a week. Remove chicken from the liquid, cut in the Chinese style, and serve cold. The sherry liquor may be kept in the refrigerator for future use.

✳ Braised Chicken with Mushrooms

✳ TUNG KU HUNG SHAO CHI

1 3-pound chicken	⅛ teaspoon pepper
15 mushrooms, soaked	2½ cups water
1 medium bamboo shoot	2 stalks scallions, cut into
2 water chestnuts	1-inch sections
1 tablespoon soy sauce	
enough oil for deep frying	Thickening:
5 slices ginger	2 teaspoons cornstarch
1 teaspoon salt	mixed with
½ teaspoon sugar	3 tablespoons water

Slice the mushrooms, bamboo shoots and water chestnuts into shreds. Cut the chicken in half and rub the soy sauce inside and out. Heat a deep frying pan with about 1 inch of oil; when it is very hot lower the chicken into the oil and fry on each side for 2 minutes. Drain the chicken and set aside. Drain the oil. In the oily pan sauté the ginger with the salt for 1 minute, add water, mushrooms, scallions, water chestnuts, bamboo shoots, sugar and pepper. Place the chicken in this mixture and cover. Lower the heat and simmer for 15 minutes.

Remove the chicken and chop into pieces 1½ inches by 1 inch and arrange on a serving dish. Stir the thickening into the gravy and when it is clear and thick pour the whole mixture over the chicken and serve at once.

✻ Red-Cooked Chicken with Chestnuts

✻ LI TZU HUNG SHAO CHI

1 4-pound chicken
2 tablespoons oil
1 small onion, sliced
4 mushrooms, soaked and
    stemmed
1 slice ginger, chopped
1 teaspoon salt
1 teaspoon sugar

20 chestnuts, shelled and
    blanched
3 cups hot water
Thickening:
1 tablespoon cornstarch
mixed with
4 tablespoons soy sauce
2 tablespoons sherry

Remove the legs and wings from the chicken and chop into 1½-inch pieces. Cut the chicken in half from the back with a cleaver, and chop each half again into six pieces, bone and all. Heat a pan with the oil and when it is hot, add the onion and sauté till it becomes transparent. Add the chicken pieces and brown well. Cut the mushrooms in half and sauté with the chicken. Season with salt, sugar and ginger and stir once or twice. Pour the thickening in slowly, stirring until it becomes smooth and thick. Add the chestnuts and the water slowly. Bring to a boil and cover. Lower the heat and simmer for about 1 hour or until the chicken is tender. Arrange chicken and chestnuts in a shallow bowl and pour the gravy over it. Serve immediately.

✳ Braised Chicken with Sweet Peppers

✳ CH'ING CHIAO HUNG SHAO CHI

2 small green peppers	2 slices ginger
1 2½-pound chicken	3 tablespoons oil
3 tablespoons soy sauce	1 teaspoon salt
2 tablespoons sherry	½ cup water
1 stalk scallion, cut into 1-inch sections	

Wash the peppers, discard the seeds and cut into ¾-inch squares. Chop the chicken Chinese style: remove the wings and legs and cut each limb into three; cut the chicken in half through the backbone and each half into six pieces, about 1½-inch squares. Pour the soy sauce, sherry, scallions and ginger over the chicken and let it marinate for about 10 minutes, turning the pieces occasionally.

Heat a pan with the oil; when it is very hot add the chicken and the liquid and stir for 2 minutes. Turn the heat high and add the salt and water slowly. When it boils, lower the heat, cover and simmer for 2 minutes. Add the green peppers and cook for another 3 minutes, stirring occasionally. Serve on a flat platter immediately.

✳ Chicken with Pepper Sauce

✳ LA CHIANG CHI

1 5-pound chicken
2 quarts water

Sauce:
  4 tablespoons soy sauce
  ½ teaspoon cayenne pepper
  ½ teaspoon hot pepper powder
  3 tablespoons chicken fat

Wash the chicken, put in a heavy saucepan and cover with water. Bring to a boil and turn down the heat and simmer for 2 hours. Remove from the water, drain and put immediately in the refrigerator. When it is cold and just before serving cut the chicken up Chinese style: cut in half through the backbone, then into pieces 2 inches square, cutting through the bone. Arrange on a flat dish, skin side up. Mix the ingredients for the sauce together and heat. Pour over chicken, stirring well.

✳ Deep-Fried Chicken

✳ CHA CHI

1 2-pound chicken
enough water to cover chicken
enough oil for deep frying
1 slice ginger
1 stalk scallion, cut into 1-inch
    sections

Marinade:
  3 teaspoons sherry
  5 teaspoons soy sauce
  3 teaspoons cornstarch

Place the chicken in a saucepan and add enough water to cover. Bring to a boil, turn down the heat and simmer for about 1 hour. Remove chicken from the broth and bone it, cutting the meat into shreds about 2 inches long, and allow it to cool. Coat the chicken with the marinade and allow it to stand for a few minutes. Heat a pan and add enough oil for deep frying. Add ginger and scallions. When this is hot, fry the pieces of chicken for about 1 minute or until brown and crisp. Serve immediately.

✳ Paper-Wrapped Chicken

✳ CHIH PAO CHI

1 3-pound chicken	Marinade:
2 cups oil	2 tablespoons soy sauce
2 stalks scallions, cut into 1-inch sections	1 tablespoon sherry
	1 teaspoon chopped ginger
20 squares of wax paper 4 by 4 inches	1 teaspoon salt
	¼ teaspoon pepper
	½ teaspoon sugar

Bone the chicken, remove and discard the skin. Cut the chicken meat into slices about 1½ inches long and 1 inch wide. Blend together the mixture for the marinade and add to the chicken. Allow it to marinate for 30 minutes. Place 2 pieces of chicken and a piece of scallion on each square of wax paper and wrap the package securely, envelope fashion. Heat a pan with about 1 inch of oil, and when it is very hot fry the wrapped chicken for about 2½ minutes. Drain the packages well and serve very hot on a platter. The paper is to be unwrapped by the diner himself at table.

✳ Curried Chicken

✳ CHIA LI CHI

1 3-pound chicken	1 teaspoon crushed red pepper
3 tablespoons oil	1 teaspoon salt
3 large onions, sliced	1 no. 2 can tomatoes
3 tablespoons curry powder	1 cup soup stock
1 teaspoon chili powder	

Cut the chicken into small pieces, Chinese style, and set it aside. Heat a pan with the oil and sauté the onions over medium heat until they brown. Turn off the heat and let the pan cool for a few minutes. Add the curry powder and sauté with the onions, chili powder, crushed red pepper and salt and stir for about 10 minutes. Add chicken and brown it well, pour in the can of tomatoes and bring it to a boil. Add enough soup stock to barely cover the chicken and bring to a boil again. Lower the heat and simmer for 1½ hours. Serve with rice.

✳ Frogs' Legs Meat and Chicken

✳ CH'AO T'IEN CHI

½ pound chicken meat, cut into ½-inch cubes
¼ pound frogs' legs meat, cut into ½-inch cubes
2 teaspoons sherry
1 teaspoon salt
2 tablespoons cornstarch
¼ cup oil
1 slice ginger, chopped fine

2 stalks scallions, chopped fine
4 fresh mushrooms, sliced
½ cup chicken stock
1 teaspoon soy sauce

Thickening:
2 tablespoons cornstarch mixed with
4 tablespoons water

Season the chicken and frogs' legs meat with the sherry, salt and cornstarch. Heat a pan with the oil and when it is hot add the ginger and scallions and stir once. Add the meat and mushrooms and sauté for 1 minute. Add the chicken stock and soy sauce and stir once or twice. Add the thickening to the pan and when it becomes smooth and thick, serve very hot on a shallow dish.

✳ Diced Chicken with Almonds

✳ HSING JEN CHI TING

2 cups diced chicken	1 cup boiling water
3 tablespoons oil	½ cup toasted almonds
1 teaspoon salt	
2 tablespoons soy sauce	Thickening:
1 cup peas	1 tablespoon cornstarch
1 cup diced celery	mixed with
½ cup canned mushrooms	¼ cup cold water

Heat a pan with the oil and salt and when it is very hot add the chicken and sauté for 3 minutes. Season with soy sauce and stir well. Add the peas, celery, mushrooms and water very slowly and stir well. Cover the pan and cook for about 4 minutes. Add the thickening and lower the heat and when the gravy thickens and becomes clear, remove from the heat, and transfer into a shallow plate. Sprinkle with toasted almonds. Serve very hot.

✳ Chicken Sautéed with Peppers

✳ LA CHIAO CH'AO CHI

¾ pound chicken meat, diced	3 teaspoons vegetable paste
1 teaspoon salt	(Hoisin)
1 teaspoon cornstarch	2 mushrooms, soaked and diced
2 teaspoons sherry	2 small green peppers, diced
½ cup oil	1 red chili, diced
	1 bamboo shoot, diced

Mix the salt, cornstarch and sherry together and coat the chicken with it. Heat a pan, add half of the oil and when it is very hot sauté the chicken for 2 minutes. Remove the chicken and drain it. Reheat the pan and add the remainder of the oil. Sauté the vegetable paste for 1 minute and then add the mushrooms, peppers, chili and bamboo shoot and sauté for another minute.

Add the chicken, and stir well into the mixture for 1 minute or till the chicken becomes hot. Remove from the heat and serve immediately.

❋ Chicken with Lichees

❋ LI CHIH CH'AO CHI

Chicken balls:
1 pound chicken meat, chopped fine
3 tablespoons chopped onion
6 water chestnuts, chopped fine
6 mushrooms, soaked and chopped
2 tablespoons cornstarch
½ teaspoon salt
2 tablespoons soy sauce
1 teaspoon sherry
2 egg whites, stiffly beaten

enough oil for deep frying
½ cup lichee syrup
½ cup chicken stock
1 stalk scallion cut into 1-inch sections
1 can lichees, drained

Thickening:
2 tablespoons soy sauce
mixed with
2 tablespoons cornstarch

Mix all the ingredients for the chicken balls together and form into balls the size of a small walnut. Heat a pan filled up to 1 inch of oil and when it is very hot add the chicken balls and fry till they are golden brown. Remove and drain them on absorbent paper. Reheat the pan with 1 tablespoon oil, the lychee syrup and chicken stock and the thickening mixture. Stir for a few seconds, add the chicken balls, lichees and scallion. Heat thoroughly and serve on a shallow platter immediately.

❋ Peppered Chicken

❋ LA-TZU CHI

4 half chicken breasts, diced
1 tablespoon cornstarch

2 tablespoons soy sauce
enough oil for deep frying

2 *green peppers*
1 *small red pepper*
2 *cups diced onion*
2 *tablespoons oil*
1 *clove garlic, minced*

Sauce mixture:
  2 *tablespoons cornstarch*
  3 *tablespoons soy sauce*
  1 *teaspoon sugar*
  ½ *teaspoon salt*
  ¼ *cup stock*

Coat the diced chicken with a mixture of soy sauce and corn-starch and set it aside for a few minutes. Heat a pan with enough oil for deep frying and when it is hot add the chicken and fry until golden brown. Remove from the pan and drain. Pour all but 2 tablespoons oil from the pan and set aside.

Remove the seeds from the green and hot peppers and dice and mix with the onions. Blend the sauce mixture and add to the vegetables. Heat the pan with the oil and when it is hot add garlic and sauté the vegetables for about 2 minutes and then remove. Slowly add the chicken and when it is very hot, turn onto a hot shallow dish and serve immediately.

✳ Chicken with Pineapple

✳ PO LO CHI

4 *half chicken breasts*
enough water to cover meat
2 *slices canned pineapple*
4 *tablespoons oil*
1 *cup sliced celery cabbage*
1 *cup sliced celery*
½ *cup peeled and diced water*
    chestnuts
½ *cup sliced bamboo shoots*

1½ *teaspoons salt*
  2 *teaspoons sugar*
  ½ *teaspoon pepper*
2½ *cups water*

Thickening:
  3 *teaspoons cornstarch*
mixed with
  3 *tablespoons water*

Put the chicken in a saucepan, cover with water, bring to a boil and simmer for 20 minutes. Remove from the water and when cool remove the skin and slice against the grain into ¼-inch slices.

Cut each pineapple slice into 10 chunks and set aside. Heat a pan with the oil, and when it is hot add the cabbage, celery, water chestnuts and bamboo shoots and sauté for 2 minutes, stirring constantly. Add the chicken, salt, sugar and pepper and slowly the water. Cover the pan and cook over medium heat for 6 minutes. Add the pineapple and the thickening and when the sauce is hot and thick turn onto a platter and serve at once.

* Chicken Velvet

* CHI JUNG

1 cup chicken breasts, chopped fine	Sauce:
2 teaspoons cornstarch	1 cup chicken stock
½ teaspoon salt	1 teaspoon sherry
10 egg whites	½ teaspoon salt
½ cup water	1 tablespoon cornstarch
4 tablespoons oil	

Blend the sauce mixture together and heat till it becomes thick and clear. Set aside and warm up just before serving.

Grind the chicken in a mortar with a pestle for about 15 minutes till it looks like a paste, removing all tendons. Add the cornstarch, salt and 2 unbeaten egg whites slowly. Add the water, a drop at a time, mixing well after each drop, making sure that the mixture does not separate. Beat the remaining egg whites till very stiff and fold into the chicken mixture.

Heat the pan with the oil and when it is hot add the chicken mixture. Remove from the heat immediately, and beat the mixture rapidly so that the oil is well absorbed. Return the pan to the heat for about 10 seconds or until the mixture starts to set. Drain the oil from the chicken in a sieve and arrange on a platter. Heat the sauce mixture and pour over the chicken and serve immediately.

❊ Chicken Agar-agar Salad

❊ LENG PAN CHI SSU

4 half chicken breasts
⅓ package agar-agar

Sauce:
¼ cup soy sauce
2 tablespoons sesame seed oil
2 tablespoons vinegar
1 teaspoon salt
¼ teaspoon cayenne pepper

Cut the agar-agar into 2-inch sections and soak in cold water for 2 hours, changing the water two or three times within this period. Drain well.

Boil the chicken for about 20 minutes. When cold, bone and shred into 2-inch pieces and season with a little salt. Mix well with the agar-agar.

Blend the ingredients for the sauce and pour over the chicken and let it marinate for about ½ hour. Serve cold.

OTHER BIRDS

✳ *Turkey à la Chinoise*

✳ SHAO HUO CHI

1 10-pound turkey	¼ teaspoon pepper
12 cups water	4 stalks scallions
3 cups soy sauce	8 slices ginger
1 cup sherry	1 tablespoon sesame seed oil
3 tablespoons sugar	½ head lettuce
1 tablespoon salt	

Put 12 cups water in a very large cooking vessel and add the soy
sauce, sherry, sugar, salt, pepper, scallions and ginger and bring
to a fast boil. Lower the turkey into this liquid and boil for
about 40 minutes. Transfer the turkey carefully to a roasting pan
and pour 2½ cups of the liquid over the turkey.

Preheat the oven to 450 degrees and roast the turkey for about

1 hour, basting every ten minutes. Turn the heat up to 550 degrees and pour sesame seed oil over the turkey and roast for another 15 minutes.

Cut off the breast whole and cut across the grain into pieces 1½ by ½ inch and place on a bed of lettuce, skin side upward.

This turkey may also be served whole and carved Western style.

✳ Braised Pheasant

✳ HUNG SHAO CHIH CHI

1 4-pound pheasant	3 slices ginger
2 tablespoons oil	1 stalk scallion, cut into
3 tablespoons sherry	1-inch sections
3 tablespoons soy sauce	1 cup chicken stock
	1 teaspoon sugar

Cut the pheasant into small pieces in the Chinese manner: chop through the backbone, and then cut each half into about six pieces complete with the bone. Heat pan with the oil and when it is hot add the pheasant and sauté for about 5 minutes, stirring constantly. Add the sherry and stir, and add the soy sauce, ginger, scallions and the stock slowly. When it comes to a boil, turn down the heat, cover and simmer for 30 minutes. Add the sugar, stir once or twice, cover and simmer for another 10 minutes. Serve in shallow bowl.

✳ Mandarin Style Squab

✳ HUNG SHAO KO-TZU

2 squabs	6 water chestnuts, peeled and
enough oil for deep frying	halved
10 mushrooms, soaked and	1 teaspoon sugar
halved	2 slices ginger
10 chestnuts, shelled and	1 tablespoon soy sauce
blanched	1 cup sherry
6 jujubes, peeled and halved	1 teaspoon salt
	1½ cups boiling chicken stock

Heat a deep pan and fill up to 2 inches of oil and when it is very hot, lower the squabs into it and fry for 2 minutes or until they are golden brown. Remove from the oil and rinse them in cold water. Place squabs in a casserole and add the mushrooms, chestnuts, jujubes, water chestnuts, sugar, ginger, soy sauce, sherry, salt and chicken stock. Preheat the oven to 350 degrees and cook the casserole from about 35 to 45 minutes or until the meat is ready to fall apart at the touch of a chopstick. Serve in the casserole.

✳ Savory Squabs

✳ CHA KO-TZU

4 large squabs
3 cups soy sauce
3 cups water
¾ cup sugar
1 tablespoon powdered
    cinnamon

1 clove anise
4 cups oil
3 stalks scallions, chopped
celery salt
pepper-and-salt mix

Mix the soy sauce, water, sugar, cinnamon and anise in a sauce-pan and bring to a boil; turn off the heat. Wash the squabs well and lower into this mixture. Bring the liquid to barely simmering point and reduce the heat. Simmer very slowly for 30 minutes. Remove the squabs very carefully with a draining spoon and set them aside. Heat a deep frying pan with the oil, and when it is very hot lower the squabs into the boiling fat and fry for about 2 minutes, or until the skin is very crisp. Drain them on absorbent paper for a few seconds, cut them into quarters, arrange on a shallow platter and sprinkle with scallions. Serve with side dishes of celery salt or pepper-and-salt mix.

✳ Broiled Squabs

✳ K'AO KO-TZU

2 squabs	5 tablespoons melted chicken
½ teaspoon dry mustard	fat
1 teaspoon sugar	2 tablespoons soy sauce
1 slice ginger, chopped	6 tablespoons sherry

Mix the mustard, sugar, ginger, chicken fat, soy sauce and sherry in a small pan, bring to a boil and simmer for about 2 minutes, stirring occasionally. Set it aside.

Split the squabs through the center of the breast and turn them over, back upward, so that they will be flat. Place them on a rack in a roasting pan and pour the sauce mixture over them. Broil them under medium heat, basting frequently, for about 20 to 30 minutes or until the skin is brown and crisp. Cut each squab into 4 pieces and serve very hot on a shallow plate.

✳ Squab with Oyster Sauce

✳ HAO YU KO-TZU

2 squabs	1 teaspoon sherry
1 teaspoon soy sauce	1½ cups water
2 tablespoons oil	
½ teaspoon salt	Thickening:
3 tablespoons oyster sauce	1½ teaspoons cornstarch
1 teaspoon sugar	mixed with
¼ teaspoon pepper	3 tablespoons water

Cut the squabs in half through the backbone and rub them with soy sauce inside and out. Heat a pan with the oil and salt, and when it is hot sauté the squabs for about 2 minutes. Pour the oyster sauce over them and add the sugar, pepper, sherry and water. Cover the pan and continue to cook for 2 minutes, and then turn the squabs and cook for another 2 minutes. Remove the squabs, chop them into bite-sized pieces and arrange in a shallow dish. Keep hot. Mix the ingredients for the thickening and add to the gravy and when it is smooth and thick pour over the squabs and serve immediately.

✳ Minced Squab

✳ KO SUNG

1 cup minced squab meat	3 tablespoons soy sauce
4 tablespoons oil	1 teaspoon sugar
½ teaspoon salt	2 tablespoons sherry
2 stalks celery, minced	½ cup chicken stock
6 water chestnuts, peeled and minced	dash of pepper
4 mushrooms, soaked and minced	Thickening:
1 bamboo shoot, minced	1 teaspoon cornstarch mixed with
1 stalk scallion, minced	3 tablespoons water

Heat a pan with 1 tablespoon oil and sauté the squab meat for 1 minute. Remove it and set aside. Reheat the pan and add the remaining oil and salt. Add the celery, mushrooms, water chestnuts, bamboo shoot, scallion and sauté for about 10 seconds. Add the soy sauce, sugar and sherry and slowly the chicken stock. Bring to a boil, lower the heat and simmer for 1 minute. Add the thickening and when it is thick add the meat and cook for 10 seconds. Make a bed with lettuce leaves on a serving plate and pour the minced squab over it, season with pepper and serve.

✳ Fried Quail

✳ CHA AN CH'UN

4 quails
enough oil for deep frying
pepper-and-salt mix

Marinade:
1 tablespoon soy sauce
2 teaspoons sugar
1 tablespoon sherry
2 slices ginger, chopped

Wash the quails and pat dry with a cloth. Mix the ingredients for the marinade and rub over the birds. Pour the remainder of the liquid over the birds and set them aside for about 30 minutes to absorb the flavor.

Heat the pan and fill up to 1 inch of oil and when it is very hot lower the birds in it and fry until they are golden brown. Cut in half and serve with side dishes of pepper-and-salt mix.

✳ Minced Quail

✳ AN CH'UN SUNG

2 quails
8 ounces pork

Seasoning:
1 tablespoon soy sauce
1 tablespoon cornstarch
1 teaspoon salt

1 tablespoon oil
4 bamboo shoots, diced
8 water chestnuts, diced fine
½ head lettuce
10 almonds, toasted and diced

Remove the heads and feet from the quails and set them aside for decoration. Bone the birds and mince the meat with the pork. Mix thoroughly with the seasoning and let stand for a few minutes. Heat a pan with the oil and when it is hot sauté the bamboo shoots and water chestnuts for 30 seconds. Add the minced meat and sauté the mixture for about 2 minutes or until the meat is well done, stirring constantly.

Make a bed of lettuce leaves on a serving plate and pour the meat over it and sprinkle with almonds. If desired, decorate with heads and feet of the quail after frying them.

✳ Fried Snipe

✳ CHA YÜ

6 snipes
enough oil for deep frying
½ head lettuce
pepper-and-salt mix

Marinade:
1 tablespoon soy sauce
2 teaspoons sugar
1 tablespoon sherry
2 slices ginger, chopped fine

Wash the snipes and dry with a cloth. Mix the ingredients for the marinade together, rub it over the birds and let them stand for 30 minutes. Heat a deep frying pan and add enough oil to cover the birds. When it is very hot, lower the birds slowly into the oil and fry till they are golden brown. Serve the snipe on a bed of lettuce leaves, and with side dishes of pepper-and-salt mix.

PORK

* Taiwan Pork

* TAIWAN JO

3 cups pork, diced into ½-inch
  cubes
3 tablespoons oil
2 cups chopped onion
1 pound celery cabbage, finely
  shredded

3 tablespoons soy sauce
½ teaspoon sugar
2 slices ginger, shredded fine
½ teaspoon salt
2 cups sliced green peppers

Heat a pan with the oil and when it is very hot add the pork and
sauté for about 4 minutes. Add the onion and continue to sauté
for another minute. Add the cabbage and stir 3 or 4 times. Now
add the soy sauce, sugar, ginger, salt and green peppers. Stir for
another 2 minutes and when it is very hot, turn onto a shallow
bowl and serve immediately.

✳ Red-Cooked Pork Shoulder

✳ HUNG SHAO CHOU-TZU

1 6-pound pork shoulder	4 slices ginger
2 cups water	4 stalks scallions
¼ cup sherry	1 tablespoon sugar
1 cup soy sauce	

Wash the pork well, pulling off any hairs there may be on the skin, and place the meat, skin side up, in a heavy saucepan with the water. Turn the heat high and when the water boils, pour the sherry over the pork, followed by the soy sauce. Place the ginger and scallions in the liquid, cover the pot and lower the heat and simmer for one hour. Turn the meat and simmer for another hour. Turn the meat again and add the sugar and cook another half hour. The meat should now be tender enough to give way with chopsticks. Serve in a deep bowl with the gravy poured over it.

✳ Szechuan Pork

✳ CH'UAN JO

1 2-pound center cut pork rib roast	2 tablespoons soy jam
3 cups water	4 slices ginger
2 tablespoons oil	1 teaspoon sugar
½ clove garlic, crushed	½ teaspoon tabasco sauce
1 stalk scallion, cut into 1-inch sections	

Put the pork in a saucepan and cover with water. Bring to a boil and simmer for an hour. Remove and allow it to cool. Remove the bones and slice the meat against the grain ½ inch thick. Cut this into sections 2 inches long and 1 inch wide.

Heat a pan with the oil and when it is very hot add the garlic and stir once or twice. Add the meat and sauté for about 2 minutes. Add the scallion, soy jam, ginger, sugar and tabasco sauce. Sauté for 2 minutes, stirring constantly, and serve very hot on a shallow dish.

✳ Fresh Bacon with Pea Starch Noodles

✳ CHU JO FEN T'IAO

¼ pound pea starch noodles	2 tablespoons sherry
1½ pounds fresh bacon	1 teaspoon salt
3 cups water	4 slices ginger
4 tablespoons soy sauce	1 teaspoon sugar

Add the noodles to a large saucepan of boiling water and cook for 30 minutes. Turn off heat and let soak for another hour.

Cut the meat into 1½-inch cubes and put in another pan with 1 cup of water. Bring to a boil, add the soy sauce, sherry, salt and ginger. Lower the heat, cover, and simmer for an hour. Drain the noodles and add to the meat. When it comes to the boil again, slowly add the remaining 2 cups of boiling water and sugar and continue to simmer for another hour. Serve very hot in a deep bowl.

✳ Steamed Pork with Ground Rice (Method I)

✳ MI FEN JO

1 pound fresh bacon	Marinade:
½ pound ground rice	3 tablespoons soy sauce
	1 tablespoon sherry

Cut the pork into pieces 2 inches long, 1 inch wide and about ½ inch thick and soak them in the marinade for about 15 minutes. Brown the ground rice in a heavy pan over low heat for 3 or 4 minutes. Remove and cool. Dredge each piece of meat thoroughly in this ground rice and arrange in an oven-proof bowl.

Place a rack in a pan filled up to 2 inches of boiling water. Place the bowl on this rack and steam for about 1½ hours. While steaming turn the meat several times and, if it becomes too dry, add a few drops of sherry mixed with soy sauce. Serve very hot

✳ Steamed Pork with Ground Rice (Method II)

✳ MI FEN JO

1½ pounds fresh bacon
enough water to cover pork
1 cup rice flour
4 slices ginger, finely chopped
1 stalk scallion, finely chopped
½ teaspoon salt

½ teaspoon sugar
4 teaspoons soy sauce
2 teaspoons sesame oil
½ cup water
2 large slices ginger
2 stalks scallion

Place the rice flour in a bowl and mix with chopped ginger, scallion, salt, sugar, soy sauce, oil and water; blend into a smooth paste.

Place the pork in a saucepan and cover with water. Bring to a boil and cook for 40 minutes. Remove the meat and cut into ½-inch slices vertically. Coat each slice with the rice paste, and arrange in a bowl vertically, skin surface downward on the bottom of the bowl, so that it will be smooth when turned out. Place the ginger and scallions on top of the meat. Have a rack ready in a steaming pan and place the bowl on it. Cover and steam for 2½ hours. When ready, turn meat carefully onto a shallow bowl and serve immediately.

✳ Red-Cooked Meat with Turnips

✳ LO PO HUNG SHAO JO

2 *pounds fresh bacon*	1 *teaspoon salt*
1½ *cups water*	4 *slices ginger*
4 *tablespoons soy sauce*	1 *pound turnips*
2 *tablespoons sherry*	1 *teaspoon sugar*

Cut the meat into 1½-inch cubes and place in a heavy saucepan with the water. Bring to a boil and add the soy sauce, sherry, salt and ginger. Lower the heat and simmer for an hour. Peel the turnips and cut them about the same size as the meat with the rolling cut. Add to the meat and continue to cook over low heat for ½ hour. Add the sugar and cook for another ½ hour. Serve very hot in a deep bowl.

✳ Sweet and Sour Spare Ribs

✳ T'ANG TS'U P'AI KU

2½ *pounds spare ribs cut into*	*Sauce:*
1-inch lengths	3 *tablespoons sugar*
2 *cups water*	3 *tablespoons vinegar*
4 *tablespoons soy sauce*	2 *tablespoons cornstarch*
1 *teaspoon salt*	½ *cup water*
1 *teaspoon sugar*	
2 *tablespoons sherry*	

Heat a pan, add 2 cups of water, the ribs, soy sauce and salt. When it boils turn down the heat and simmer for 1 hour. Transfer the ribs and liquid into a saucepan, and add the sugar and sherry. Turn the heat high and continue to cook till the liquid is all evaporated. Blend the ingredients for the sauce and pour slowly over the ribs. Continue to cook for about 2 minutes or until the sauce becomes thick and smooth. Place the ribs on a flat dish, pour the sauce on top and serve at once.

✳ Sweet and Sour Pork

✳ T'ANG TS'U CHU JO

1 pound pork shoulder, cubed
    into ¾-inch pieces
enough oil for deep frying

Batter:
  1 egg
  ½ cup flour
  ½ teaspoon salt
  4 tablespoons water

Sauce:
  1 cup pineapple cubes
  1 green pepper, cut into
    ¾-inch squares
  ½ cup vinegar
  ¼ cup brown sugar
  ¾ cup water
  1 tablespoon molasses

Thickening:
  2 tablespoons cornstarch
  mixed with
  ¼ cup water

Heat a deep frying pan with the oil. Mix the batter, dip the pork cubes into this mixture and drop into the boiling fat. When they brown, remove them and drain on absorbent paper. Mix the ingredients for the sauce in a pan and bring slowly to a boil, stirring constantly. Pour the thickening into the sauce, and when it becomes thick and smooth, add the meat and mix well. When it is very hot, turn into a shallow bowl and serve immediately.

✳ Diced Pork with Green Peas

✳ CH'ING TOU JO TING

¼ pound pork, diced fine
1 tablespoon oil
1 cup peas
1 cup water
1 teaspoon salt
⅛ teaspoon pepper

Thickening:
  2 teaspoons cornstarch
  mixed with
  ¼ cup water

Heat pan with the oil and when it is hot sauté the meat for 2 minutes. Slowly add the peas and stir for 2 minutes longer. Add the water, salt and pepper. Cover, lower the heat and cook for 6 minutes. Add the thickening to the pan and stir till the gravy becomes thick and smooth. Turn onto a shallow dish and serve immediately.

❋ Sliced Pork Sautéed with Vegetables

❋ CH'ING TS'AI CH'AO JO P'IEN

2 cups sliced pork
2 tablespoons oil
1 cup chopped onion
12 mushrooms, soaked and cut
    into strips
1 cup shredded celery
2 cups sliced green peppers
4 tablespoons soy sauce
1 cup bean sprouts

½ cup sliced water chestnuts
1 slice ginger, chopped fine
½ cup mushroom water

Thickening:
2 tablespoons cornstarch
mixed with
4 tablespoons water

Heat a pan with the oil and when it is hot sauté the pork for 10 minutes. Add the onions, stir once or twice, add the mushrooms, stir, and add the celery and green peppers and cook for about 10 seconds. Add the soy sauce, bean sprouts, water chestnuts, ginger and the mushroom water. Stir quickly and add the thickening. When the gravy becomes thick and smooth, turn onto a hot shallow dish and serve immediately.

❋ Sliced Pork with Green Peppers

❋ CH'ING CHIAO JO P'IEN

1½ pounds pork
4 green peppers
4 tablespoons oil

¼ teaspoon pepper
½ teaspoon salt

Marinade:
2½ *tablespoons soy sauce*
 1 *tablespoon sherry*
 1 *teaspoon sugar*

1 *teaspoon salt*
1 *tablespoon cornstarch*
2 *tablespoons water*

Slice the pork thinly into pieces about 1 inch square. Blend the ingredients for the marinade and coat the meat with this mixture; marinate for about 15 minutes. Wash the peppers, discarding the seeds, and cut them into ½-inch squares. Heat a pan with 2 tablespoons oil and when it is hot add the peppers and sauté for 2 minutes, stirring constantly. Remove them from the pan and set aside. Add enough oil to the pan to make 2 tablespoons and when it is hot add the meat and sauté for 1 minute. Add the peppers and the remainder of the marinade and stir well. When it becomes very hot and thick add the pepper and salt to taste. Turn onto a shallow dish and serve at once.

✳ Fried Pork Balls

✳ CHA JO WAN

1½ *pounds minced pork*
 1 *small onion, minced*
 ¼ *cup chopped celery*
 ¼ *mushrooms, soaked and*
    chopped

½ *teaspoon salt*
⅛ *teaspoon pepper*

enough oil for deep frying
pepper-and-salt mix

Mix all the ingredients well together and shape into balls the size of a small walnut.

Heat a pan and fill up to 1 inch of oil. When it is very hot, lower the balls into the pan and fry till they are very brown outside and thoroughly cooked inside. Cut one open to make sure that the meat is not pink. Serve the balls on a shallow dish with side dishes of pepper-and-salt mix.

✳ Pork with Bamboo Shoots

✳ TUNG SUN CH'AO JO

½ pound pork, sliced
4 tablespoons oil
2 cups sliced bamboo shoots
¼ cup water

Marinade:
2 tablespoons soy sauce
½ teaspoon salt
2 tablespoons sherry
1 tablespoon cornstarch

Heat a pan with 2 tablespoons oil and when it is hot add the bamboo shoots and sauté for 2 minutes. Remove from the pan. Mix the ingredients for the marinade and coat the sliced pork with this mixture. Reheat the pan with the remaining 2 tablespoons oil and sauté the pork for about 2 minutes. Add the shoots and the water and bring to a boil. Simmer for 1 minute, stirring all the time. Serve very hot in a shallow dish.

✳ Pork Sautéed with Snow Peas

✳ HSUËH TOU CH'AO JO

2 tablespoons oil
¼ pound sliced pork
¼ teaspoon salt
1 teaspoon sherry
¼ pound snow peas
½ cup water
¼ teaspoon pepper

Thickening:
1 teaspoon cornstarch
mixed with
3 tablespoons water
1 teaspoon soy sauce
½ teaspoon sugar

Heat a pan with the oil and salt and when it is very hot add the pork and sauté for 2 minutes. Add the sherry and snow peas and stir 2 or 3 times. Add the water, cover and cook for 2 minutes more. Add the thickening and when it is smooth and thick, sprinkle with the pepper and serve in a shallow dish immediately.

* Pickled Mustard Greens with Pork

* CHA TS'AI CHU JO

1 *pound pickled mustard greens*	¼ *pound pork, sliced thin*
1 *slice ginger*	½ *cup soup stock*
1 *tablespoon sherry*	
1 *teaspoon soy sauce*	*Thickening:*
3 *tablespoons vinegar*	1 *teaspoon cornstarch*
3 *tablespoons sugar*	*mixed with*
1 *tablespoon oil*	2 *tablespoons water*

Wash the mustard greens, squeeze out all the water and cut into 1-inch pieces. Mix the ginger, sherry and soy together, and in another bowl mix the vinegar and sugar. Heat a pan, add the mustard greens and stir them for 2 or 3 minutes till they are dry. Remove from the pan and set aside. Add the oil to the pan and when it is very hot add the pork and sauté till it is brown. Pour the sherry mixture over the pork and stir for 30 seconds. Add the greens and the stock, mix well with the pork and cook for 2 minutes. Slowly pour in the vinegar preparation and continue to cook, stirring constantly. Add the thickening and when it is smooth and thick serve in a shallow bowl.

* Steamed Pork with Salted Cabbage

* HSIEN TS'AI CHEN CHU JO

1 *pound pork, sliced thin*	½ *cup salted cabbage,*
1 *teaspoon cornstarch*	*chopped fine*
1 *teaspoon oil*	2 *tablespoons chopped water*
2 *teaspoons soy sauce*	*chestnuts*

Mix the cornstarch, oil and soy sauce together in a heatproof bowl and coat the meat with this mixture. Mix the cabbage with the meat and sprinkle with the water chestnuts.

Place a rack in a large saucepan filled up to 2 inches of boiling water. Place the bowl on the rack and cover the pan. Steam for 30 minutes and serve very hot in the bowl.

✳ Shredded Pork with Pea Sprouts

✳ TOU YA JO SSU

1½ pounds pork
   3 tablespoons oil
   1 pound pea sprouts

Marinade:
2½ tablespoons soy sauce
   1 tablespoon sherry
   1 teaspoon sugar
   1 teaspoon salt

Cut the meat into shreds and cover with the marinating mixture. Heat a pan with the oil and when it is hot add the pork and sauté for 2 minutes and then add the pea sprouts and the remainder of the marinade. Sauté for another 1½ minutes, stirring constantly. Serve very hot in a shallow dish.

✳ Pork Chop Suey

✳ CHU JO TSA SUI

   1 pound shredded pork
   2 tablespoons oil
   3 stalks celery
 12 fresh mushrooms, stemmed
         and shredded
 12 water chestnuts, shredded
 ½ pound pea sprouts
 ½ cup chicken stock

Thickening:
   1 tablespoon cornstarch
mixed with
   3 tablespoons water
   3 tablespoons soy sauce

 ½ teaspoon salt
 ⅛ teaspoon pepper

Heat a pan with oil and when it is very hot, sauté the meat for 1 minute. Add the celery, mushrooms, water chestnuts and pea sprouts. Stir three or four times till all the vegetables and meat are well mixed. Add the stock, cover and continue to cook for 5 minutes. Add the thickening and when it is smooth and thick add the pepper and salt. Stir once or twice and serve in a shallow bowl immediately.

✳ Hong Kong Chop Suey

✳ HSIANG KANG CHA SUI

½ pound shredded pork	¼ cup soup stock
2 tablespoons oil	1 cup pea sprouts
1 tablespoon soy sauce	⅛ teaspoon pepper
2 cups shredded celery	½ teaspoon salt
1 cup shredded onion	

Heat a pan with oil and when it is very hot add the meat and sauté for 1 minute. Add the soy sauce, celery, onion and stock; boil for 1 minute, stirring constantly. Lower the heat, cover, and continue to cook for 5 minutes. Add the pea sprouts and stir two or three times so that the vegetables are well mixed; cover again for 2 minutes, by which time the pea sprouts should be well heated. Season with pepper and salt to taste and serve immediately in a shallow dish.

✳ Lion's Head

✳ SSU TZU T'OU

1 pound ground pork	4 tablespoons soy sauce
½ pound stale bread, in small pieces	½ teaspoon salt
	⅛ teaspoon pepper
8 mushrooms, soaked and chopped fine	2 teaspoons sugar
	2 teaspoons cornstarch
12 water chestnuts, chopped fine	1 tablespoon oil
1 cup chopped onion	2 tablespoons oil
2 slices ginger, chopped fine	2 pounds celery cabbage, cut into 4-inch lengths
1 egg, well beaten	
1 teaspoon sherry	1½ cups chicken stock

Mix the pork with the bread, mushrooms, water chestnuts, onion and ginger. Add egg, sherry, soy sauce, salt, pepper, sugar, cornstarch and 1 tablespoon oil and mix thoroughly. Shape into 4 large balls. Heat pan with 2 tablespoons oil and when it is hot add the meat balls and sauté till well browned.

Cut the celery cabbage into quarters and then into 4-inch sections. Place in a large flat pan and put the meat balls on top. Add the chicken stock and simmer for 2 hours. Arrange the cabbage on a platter and the balls on top of the cabbage and pour the gravy over all. Serve at once.

✳ Steamed Pork with Shrimp Sauce

✳ HSIA YU CHEN JO

1 pound pork, sliced thin
1 tablespoon shrimp sauce

1 slice ginger, shredded fine
1 stalk scallion, cut into 1-inch sections

Place the pork in a deep ovenproof bowl and mix the shrimp sauce thoroughly with it. Add the ginger and the scallion.

Place a rack in a large saucepan filled up to 2 inches of boiling water and place the bowl on it. Cover the pan and steam for 30 minutes, or until pork is well done. Serve in the bowl.

✳ Green Pepper Stuffed with Pork

✳ CH'ING CHIAO JO

Filling:
1 pound minced pork

1 tablespoon oil
1 teaspoon salt

1½ tablespoons soy sauce
¼ teaspoon pepper
1 tablespoon cornstarch
2 stalks scallions, finely
   chopped
4 large green peppers
2 tablespoons oil
1 teaspoon salt

¼ teaspoon pepper
½ cup chicken stock

Thickening:
1 tablespoon cornstarch
mixed with
1 tablespoon soy sauce
¼ cup water

Mix the ingredients for the filling well together and set aside.
Remove the stalks from the peppers and scoop out the seeds.
Wash well and fill with the meat mixture. Heat a pan, add the
2 tablespoons oil and when hot place the peppers in it open side
up. Add the chicken stock. Cover the pan, lower the heat and
cook gently for an hour. Remove the peppers and place in a
shallow bowl. Add the thickening to the gravy in the pan and
turn up the heat, stirring constantly. When it is thick and smooth,
pour over the peppers and serve immediately.

✷ Stuffed Lotus Stem

✷ O P'IEN CHU JO

1 cup minced pork
1 tablespoon oil
1 cup chopped onion
1 slice ginger, chopped
2 tablespoons soy sauce
1 tablespoon cornstarch
10 ⅛-inch slices lotus stem

Batter:
1 egg
½ cup water
½ cup flour
¼ teaspoon salt

enough oil for deep frying

Heat pan with the oil and when it is very hot add the pork,
onion, ginger, soy sauce and cornstarch and sauté well together.
Remove the mixture to a plate. Mix the ingredients for the batter
together and set it aside. Heat the pan again and fill up to 2
inches of oil and heat till it is very hot. Spread the pork mixture
between 2 slices of lotus stem and dip in the batter till it is well

coated. Lower into the boiling oil and fry till it is golden brown. Remove from the oil and drain on absorbent paper. Serve very hot on a shallow plate.

* Minced Pork with String Beans

* SSU CHI TOU JO SUNG

1 *pound minced pork*	1½ *cups boiling water*
1 *pound green beans*	½ *head lettuce, shredded fine*
2 *tablespoons oil*	
1 *clove garlic*	*Thickening:*
2 *tablespoons soy sauce*	1 *tablespoon cornstarch*
¼ *teaspoon salt*	*mixed with*
6 *water chestnuts, chopped fine*	¼ *cup cold water*

Cut the beans into tiny even slices crosswise. Heat a pan with the oil and when it is hot add the garlic, stir once or twice, then add the pork and brown it well. Add the soy sauce, salt and water chestnuts and sauté for 2 minutes, stirring constantly. Stir in the beans, and pour the water in slowly, mixing well. Cover the pan and bring the mixture to boiling point. Turn down the heat and simmer for about 4 minutes, stirring occasionally. Add the thickening to the mixture and stir well till the sauce is thick and smooth. Place the lettuce on a warm shallow platter and pour the mixture over the leaves and serve at once.

* Minced Pork with Water Chestnuts

* PI CHI CHEN JO

1 *pound minced pork*	½ *teaspoon sugar*
6 *water chestnuts, finely*	4 *tablespoons water*
chopped	½ *teaspoon soy sauce*
1 *teaspoon cornstarch*	¼ *teaspoon pepper*
½ *teaspoon salt*	1 *tablespoon oil*

Mix all the ingredients together and place in an ovenproof serving bowl. Place a rack in a saucepan filled up to 2 inches of boiling water and place the bowl on it. Cover the pan and steam for 30 minutes. Serve very hot in the bowl.

BEEF

✻ Five Flavor Beef

✻ WU HSIANG NIU JO

4 pounds brisket of beef
4 tablespoons oil
2 cups soy sauce
2 cups water
1-inch stick cinnamon

2 cloves anise
½ cup sugar
1 tablespoon salt
1 cup sherry

Heat a deep, heavy pan with oil and when it is very hot place the whole piece of meat in it and brown on all sides. Mix the soy sauce, water, cinnamon, anise, sugar and salt in a large bowl and pour slowly over the meat. Cover the pan and when the liquid comes to a boil, turn down the heat and simmer. Baste from time to time and turn the meat every half hour. After the meat has cooked for 1½ hours, turn up the heat and add the sherry and when it comes to the boil again, turn down the heat and simmer for another ½ hour. During the last 15 minutes, turn the heat high and cook till the gravy is thickened and absorbed into the meat. The presence of sugar will thicken the liquid, therefore, you must be very careful to watch this last cooking period very carefully. Cut the meat into thick slices and pour gravy over it. Serve very hot.

✳ Red-Cooked Shin of Beef

✳ HUNG SHAO NIU NAN

2 pounds shin of beef	4 tablespoons soy sauce
2 tablespoons oil	1 teaspoon sesame seed oil
⅛ teaspoon pepper	1 teaspoon salt
2 slices ginger	2 teaspoons sugar
1 clove garlic	1 tablespoon sherry
1 stalk scallion, cut in half	enough water to cover meat

Heat a pan with oil and when it is hot add the meat and brown on both sides. Add pepper, ginger, garlic and scallion. Transfer the meat and seasoning to a saucepan and pour the soy sauce, sesame seed oil, salt, sugar and sherry over it. Add enough boiling water to cover the meat. Bring the liquid to a boil, cover and turn down the heat. Simmer slowly for 2½ hours. Remove the meat and cut into slices ¼ inch thick and arrange on a shallow dish. Pour gravy over it and serve at once.

✳ Spiced Beef

✳ HSIANG LIAO NIU JO

1 pound shin beef	2 cloves anise
1 tablespoon oil	1 teaspoon sugar

Seasoning:
3 *tablespoons soy sauce*
1 *tablespoon water*
1 *clove garlic*

1 *teaspoon sherry*
1 *teaspoon pepper*
1 *teaspoon salt*

Heat a small pan just big enough to hold the meat flat with the oil. Brown the beef on all sides, turning it carefully. Add the seasoning and when it boils turn the heat very low, cover and simmer for 10 minutes. Place the pan on an asbestos pad. Add the anise and continue to simmer for one hour. Be careful not to burn the meat. The water should not evaporate because of the steam generated in the cooking. However, if the pan becomes too dry add 1 tablespoon each of soy sauce and hot water. Add sugar, turn the meat and simmer for another hour. Remove from the pan and cut into ¼-inch slices and arrange on a platter. Pour the sauce over the meat and serve very hot.

✻ Braised Beef

✻ HUNG SHAO NIU JO

1 *pound shin beef*
1 *small tomato*
2 *tablespoons oil*
1 *tablespoon soy sauce*

1 *teaspoon sherry*
1 *clove garlic*
½ *teaspoon salt*
1 *cup chicken stock*

Cut the beef into 2-inch cubes. Cut the tomato into eighths. Heat a pan with oil and when it is hot, sauté the beef for 3 minutes. Add the soy sauce and let it simmer on a very low fire for another 15 minutes. Add the sherry, garlic and salt and stir well. Pour the stock in slowly and cover the pan and cook for another 10 minutes. Add the tomato and allow it to simmer for another 10 minutes. Serve in a bowl.

* Barbecued Beef

* K'AO NIU JO

2 pounds tenderloin beef
1 clove garlic
4 tablespoons soy sauce

2 teaspoons sugar
1 teaspoon salt

Cut the beef into 2½-inch squares and cut them into slices against the grain. Mix the garlic with the soy sauce, sugar and salt and pour it over the meat. Let the meat marinate for half an hour.

Place the beef in a pan under a medium broiler for 1½ minutes on one side and 1 minute on the other. Arrange on a shallow platter and serve at once.

* Beef Sautéed with Asparagus

* LU SUN CH'AO TS'AI

½ pound top round steak
¼ pound asparagus
2 stalks scallions
2 slices ginger
2 tablespoons oil for asparagus
3 tablespoons oil for meat

Marinade:
¼ teaspoon salt
1½ teaspoons sugar
1½ teaspoons cornstarch
⅛ teaspoon monosodium glutamate
1 tablespoon sherry
2 tablespoons soy sauce

Cut the meat into pieces 2 inches by 1 inch and slice it very thin across the grain. Mix the marinade well in a bowl, coat the meat well with it and allow to stand for 15 minutes in the mixture. Cut the scallions in half lengthwise and then into 1½-inch sections. Remove the fibrous part of the asparagus stems and slice asparagus very thin, using the rolling cut.

Heat a pan with 2 tablespoons oil and when it is very hot, add the asparagus and sauté over high heat for 2 minutes, stirring constantly, adding salt to taste. When the vegetable turns bright green, remove from the pan and set it aside. Add 3 tablespoons oil to the pan and when it is hot add the scallions, ginger, and meat and stir for 30 seconds. Return the asparagus to the pan and sauté for another minute. Turn off the heat, but continue to stir for one more minute as it is still cooking from the heat of the pan. Serve in a shallow dish immediately.

✳ Beef with Cauliflower and Snow Peas

✳ HSUËH TOU TS'AI HUA NIU JO

1 *pound beef, sliced thin*
2 *tablespoons oil*
1 *clove garlic*
4 *tablespoons chopped onion*
2 *teaspoons salt*
⅛ *teaspoon pepper*
1 *cup chicken stock*
1 *cup cauliflower flowerets*

½ *pound snow peas, stemmed*

Thickening:
 1 *tablespoon cornstarch*
mixed with
 2 *tablespoons soy sauce*
¼ *cup water*

Heat a pan with oil and add the garlic; when it is brown, remove it. Add the beef and sauté for 20 seconds, then add the onion, salt and pepper and stir for another 10 seconds. Slowly add the chicken stock, cauliflower and the snow peas. Cook over low heat for 5 minutes or until the cauliflower is cooked through but not limp. Add thickening to the pan and stir constantly, and when the sauce thickens and becomes smooth, turn the meat and vegetables into a shallow bowl and serve immediately.

✳ Beef Sautéed with Celery Cabbage

✳ PAI TS'AI CH'AO NIU JO

1 pound beef, sliced thin	½ pound celery cabbage
3 tablespoons oil	1 teaspoon sugar
1 clove garlic, crushed	2 tablespoons soy sauce
1 thick slice ginger	1 tablespoon cornstarch
1 teaspoon salt	½ cup water
¼ teaspoon pepper	

Heat pan with oil and garlic and when the garlic turns gold, remove it and discard. Sauté the meat for 2 minutes and then add the ginger, salt and pepper and stir two or three times. Remove the beef from the pan and set it aside. Shred the cabbage into 1½-inch pieces and add to the pan; sprinkle with sugar and turn the heat down very low and stir constantly for 2 minutes. Return meat to the pan, add the soy sauce and turn up the heat. Mix the vegetables and meat well, stir for 2 minutes and add the thickening. When the gravy becomes smooth and thick, serve at once in a shallow dish.

✳ Beef and Small Chinese Cabbage in Oyster Sauce

✳ HAO YU PAI TS'AI CH'AO NIU JO

1 pound filet of beef	1½ pounds small Chinese cabbage
Marinade:	2 tablespoons oil for cabbage
¼ teaspoon salt	5 tablespoons oil for meat
1 teaspoon sugar	2 slices ginger
2 tablespoons sherry	1 clove garlic
2 teaspoons cornstarch	1 stalk scallion, chopped fine
2 tablespoons water	2 tablespoons oyster sauce

Wash and cut the Chinese cabbage into quarters through the heart then into 1-inch sections and drain well. Heat a pan with 2 tablespoons oil and when it is very hot, sauté the cabbage for 3 minutes, stirring constantly. Set it aside.

Cut the beef against the grain into very thin slices, about ¾ inch wide and 1½ inches long. Mix the marinating mixture together and pour over the meat and let stand for ½ hour.

Heat pan with 5 tablespoons oil and when hot sauté the meat for 1 minute. Drain off the oil, add ginger, garlic and scallion and stir well for another minute. Add the oyster sauce and when it is well mixed stir in the cabbage. When the vegetable turns dark green take off the fire and continue to stir once or twice. Serve in a shallow dish.

✳ Beef with Green Peppers

✳ CH'ING CHIAO NIU JO

¾ pound beef, sliced
3 tablespoons oil
1 teaspoon salt
⅛ teaspoon pepper
1 stalk scallion, cut into
    ½-inch sections
1 clove garlic
3 green peppers, sliced

½ cup diced celery
1 cup chicken stock

Thickening:
  2 teaspoons cornstarch
mixed with
  1 teaspoon soy sauce
¼ cup water

Heat a pan with the oil, salt and pepper and when it is very hot, sauté the beef for 1 minute, stirring constantly. Add the scallion, garlic and green peppers. Stir once or twice and then add the celery and the chicken stock slowly. Cover the pan and turn down the heat and simmer for 10 minutes. Add the thickening to the meat, and when the gravy is thick and smooth, turn into a shallow bowl and serve immediately.

✳ Beef with Mushrooms

✳ TUNG KU NIU JO

¾ pound beef, sliced thin
2 tablespoons oil
1 teaspoon salt
⅛ teaspoon pepper
½ cup chicken stock
¾ pound mushrooms, sliced

Thickening:
2 tablespoons cornstarch
mixed with
1 tablespoon soy sauce
¼ cup water

Heat a pan with the oil, salt and pepper and when it is very hot, add the beef and sauté for 1 minute, stirring constantly. Add the stock and the mushrooms, cover and cook for 3 minutes. Add the thickening to the meat, and when it becomes thick and smooth, serve immediately in a shallow bowl.

✳ Beef with Onions

✳ YANG TS'UNG NIU JO

¼ pound beef tenderloin
¼ teaspoon baking soda

Marinade:
1 tablespoon soy sauce
1 tablespoon cornstarch
½ teaspoon oil

1 tablespoon oil for onion
½ teaspoon salt
1 onion, shredded
4 tablespoons oil
⅛ teaspoon pepper
Chinese parsley for garnishing

Slice the beef and then cut crosswise into shreds and coat with baking soda. Mix it well and set it aside for 15 minutes. Mix the marinade well together and add to the meat and let it stand for another 10 minutes.

Heat pan with the oil and when it is very hot add the salt and sauté the onion for 2 minutes. Remove the onion and set it aside. Heat the pan again with 4 tablespoons oil and when it is boiling hot, add the meat and stir quickly 4 or 5 times, being careful not to let the meat burn. Add the onion and stir again. Turn off the heat and sauté for 2 or 3 seconds, and when the onion is very hot, turn onto a shallow dish, garnish with parsley and sprinkle with pepper. Serve immediately.

✳ Beef Sautéed with Snow Peas

✳ HSUËH TOU CH'AO NIU JO

¼ *pound flank steak, sliced*
1 *pound snow peas*
2 *tablespoons oil*
1 *cup soup stock*
½ *teaspoon sugar*
⅛ *teaspoon pepper*
½ *teaspoon salt*

Thickening:
2 *tablespoons cornstarch mixed with*
¼ *cup water*

Wash the peas, stem them but leave the pods intact. Heat a pan with oil and when it is very hot, sauté the beef for a minute and then add the peas, and continue to stir for another minute. Pour the stock slowly into the pan with the sugar, salt and pepper. Mix well, cover the pan and turn down the heat and cook for 5 minutes. Add the thickening, stir into the meat, and when the gravy becomes smooth and thick, turn into a shallow bowl and serve immediately.

✳ Beef with Radishes

✳ LO PO NIU JO

½ *pound beef, sliced thin*
2 *tablespoons soy sauce*
2 *teaspoons cornstarch*
8 *radishes, sliced*

Sauce:
2 *tablespoons oil*
2 *tablespoons vinegar*
6 *tablespoons water*
4 *tablespoons sugar*
1 *tablespoon cornstarch*

Coat the beef with a mixture of the soy sauce and the cornstarch and let it stand for 10 minutes. Combine the sauce mixture and place in a saucepan. When it becomes hot, add the beef and continue to cook for 2 minutes. Add the sliced radishes, and when they become hot but not limp, remove from the heat and turn onto a shallow plate and serve immediately.

✳ Beef with String Beans

✳ SSU CHI TOU NIU JO

½ pound top round beef,
   thinly sliced
2 tablespoons oil
1½ cups boiling water
½ pound string beans
¼ cup bean water

Marinade:
2 tablespoons soy sauce
1 teaspoon sugar
1 tablespoon cornstarch
½ teaspoon salt
1 tablespoon sherry

Coat the sliced beef with the marinating mixture and let it stand for 10 minutes. String the beans and cut into 2-inch lengths. Pour the boiling water over them, and then remove the beans immediately and drain. Reserve ¼ cup of this water for later use.

Heat a pan with oil and when it is hot, add the meat and sauté for 20 seconds. Add the beans and stir for anther 20 or 30 seconds and then add the reserved bean water to the mixture. Cover, turn down the heat and simmer for 1 minute. Serve on a shallow dish immediately.

* Minced Beef with Beans

* TS'AI TOU JO SUNG

1 pound string beans
4 tablespoons oil
1 teaspoon salt
1 pound minced beef
1 onion, chopped fine
½ clove garlic

1 cup beef stock

Thickening:
3 teaspoons cornstarch
½ cup water
½ teaspoon sherry

String the beans and cut them into thin slices. Parboil them for 2 or 3 minutes and then take out of the water, drain and set aside. Heat pan with the oil and salt and when it is hot, add the beef and sauté for 30 seconds. Add the onion and garlic and continue to stir for another minute. Add the beans and mix well together with the meat and add the stock. Turn down the heat and let it simmer for 3 minutes. Blend the thickening paste and add to the meat. When it becomes smooth and thick, turn off the heat and stir once or twice. Pour the meat into a shallow bowl and serve immediately.

* Minced Beef with Salted Cabbage

* HSIEN TS'AI JO SUNG

1 cup dried salted cabbage
1 pound steak, sliced thin
1 tablespoon water
1 teaspoon oil

Marinade:
½ teaspoon cornstarch
½ teaspoon sugar
½ teaspoon soy sauce
¼ teaspoon salt
⅛ teaspoon pepper
1 teaspoon oil

Wash and soak the cabbage for 15 minutes and then slice it thin. Mix the meat with the marinating mixture and see that the slices are well coated with it, then add the cabbage and the water. Put all in a deep ovenproof bowl. Place a rack in a saucepan filled up to 2 inches of boiling water. Place the bowl on the rack and steam for ½ hour. Remove the bowl from the steamer and drop a teaspoon of oil on the meat and serve at once in the hot bowl.

✳ Minced Beef Balls with Spinach

✳ PO TS'AI NIU JO WAN

1 *pound minced beef*	1 *tablespoon oil*
2 *ounces bread crumbs*	¼ *cup water*
1 *egg*	2 *tablespoons soy sauce*
1 *teaspoon sherry*	1 *pound spinach*
½ *cup flour*	

Mix the beef with the bread crumbs, egg and sherry, and roll into balls the size of walnuts. Dredge the balls with the flour. Heat a pan with the oil and sauté balls till brown. Transfer them into a saucepan with water and soy sauce and simmer for ½ hour. Turn two or three times during this period. Wash the spinach and drain it well. Sauté in the remains of the oil from the meat for 1 minute, and then place the meat balls on top of the spinach and cook together for another 2 minutes. Make a bed of the spinach on a serving plate and place the balls on top; serve very hot.

✳ Sweet and Sour Meat Balls

✳ T'ANG TS'U NIU JO WAN

3 green peppers
1 pound minced beef

Batter:
1 egg
2 tablespoons flour
½ teaspoon salt
⅛ teaspoon pepper

½ cup oil
1½ teaspoons salt

⅓ cup chicken stock
1 slice canned pineapple cut into 8 chunks

Sauce:
2 teaspoons cornstarch
2 teaspoons soy sauce
½ cup vinegar
½ cup sugar
½ cup chicken broth

Wash peppers and discard the stems and seeds. Cut into ¾-inch squares and parboil for 2 or 3 minutes. Set them aside. Mix the batter ingredients. Shape the meat into balls the size of a walnut and dip them into the batter.

Heat a pan with oil and salt and when it is very hot, place the balls in the pan and fry for 4 minutes on one side and 3 minutes on the other. When they are brown, remove to a shallow serving bowl, set aside and keep hot. Drain the oil from the pan except for 1 tablespoon and add the chicken stock and the pineapple. Heat thoroughly for about 3 minutes over low heat and add the green peppers and continue to cook another 3 minutes. Blend the ingredients for the sauce and add to the pan. Stir constantly till the gravy thickens and becomes smooth. Pour the sauce over the meat balls and serve immediately.

LAMB

❋ Steamed Leg of Lamb

❋ CHEN YANG JO

1 pound lamb steak
enough cold water to cover meat
1 teaspoon oil

2 tablespoons soy sauce
2 cloves anise, crushed
¼ teaspoon sesame seed oil

Put the lamb steak in a saucepan and cover with cold water. Bring to a boil, turn the heat down and simmer for about 20 minutes. Drain. Heat a pan with oil and when it is hot brown the lamb for a minute or two. Cut the meat into slices about ¼ inch thick and arrange them in an ovenproof serving bowl. Add the soy sauce, a few drops of sesame seed oil and the crushed anise. Place a rack in a saucepan filled up to 2 inches of boiling water. Place the bowl on the rack, cover and steam for 15 minutes. Serve very hot.

* Lamb Sautéed with Onions

* YANG TS'UNG CH'AO YANG JO

1 *pound lean lamb, sliced thin*	2 *onions*
2 *teaspoons oil*	4 *tablespoons soy sauce*
½ *teaspoon minced ginger*	

Heat a pan with oil and when it is very hot add the ginger and the lamb. Sauté till the meat is seared, add the onions, and continue to stir till they brown. Add the soy sauce and when it starts to bubble, turn onto a flat dish and serve at once.

* Red-Cooked Lamb

* HUNG SHAO YANG JO

3 *pounds shoulder of lamb*	1 *teaspoon salt*
2 *tablespoons sherry*	1 *teaspoon sugar*
4 *tablespoons soy sauce*	2 *stalks scallions*
1 *cup boiling water*	

Cut the lamb into 1¼-inch cubes and place in a saucepan over high heat. Add sherry and soy sauce and when it begins to boil add water, salt and sugar. Cut the scallions into 1¼-inch sections and add. When the liquid reaches boiling point turn heat low and simmer for about 2 hours. Serve very hot.

* Broiled Lamb

* SHAO YANG JO

2 *pounds shoulder of lamb*	3 *teaspoons sugar*
6 *tablespoons soy sauce*	1 *teaspoon salt*
2 *cloves garlic, crushed*	

Cut the lamb into 1-inch cubes and then into slices ¼-inch thick. Add the garlic to the soy sauce, sugar and salt and marinate the meat in this mixture for 30 minutes, turning frequently. Remove the meat from the marinade and place under a very hot broiler for about 5 minutes, turning once or twice.

Serve in a shallow dish immediately.

✳ Boiled Lamb

✳ SHAO YANG JO

2 *pounds tenderloin of lamb*	¼ *cup sugar*
1 *large turnip*	2 *stalks leeks*
½ *cup soy sauce*	*enough water to barely*
½ *cup sherry*	*cover meat*
1 *teaspoon salt*	

Cut the lean meat into 1-inch cubes and place in a pan. Pour enough boiling water to half-cover the meat. Peel the turnip and place in the middle of the meat and bring the water to a boil. Skim carefully, remove the turnip and discard. Add the sherry, soy sauce and salt to taste and when it comes to a boil turn the heat low and let it simmer for about 1½ hours or till just before the meat is done. Add the sugar. Wash and cut the leeks into 1-inch lengths and add to the meat mixture. Simmer for 5 minutes longer and serve very hot in a deep bowl with gravy.

✳ Curried Lamb

✳ CHIA LI YANG JO

2 *pounds lean lamb*	3 *tablespoons curry powder*
2 *tablespoons oil*	½ *teaspoon chili powder*
3 *large onions*	1 *teaspoon salt*
4 *carrots*	2 *cups chicken stock*

Slice the lamb into thin slices about 1½ inches long and 1 inch wide and set them aside. Cut the onions into strips and the carrots into 1-inch pieces, employing the rolling cut. Heat a pan with oil and sauté the onions and carrots over medium heat till they brown. Turn off the heat and allow to cool for 2 or 3 minutes. Add the curry and continue to sauté for 3 or 4 minutes, slowly adding the chili and salt, stirring constantly for 10 minutes. Add the lamb and mix it well with the onions and carrots. Add enough stock to cover the lamb and bring it to a boil. Turn the heat low and simmer for about 1 hour and correct the seasoning with pepper and salt. Serve with boiled rice.

✳ Lamb with String Beans

✳ SSU CHI TOU CH'AO YANG JO

1 *pound lean lamb*
1 *pound string beans*
2 *tablespoons oil*
1 *teaspoon salt*
⅛ *teaspoon pepper*
1 *cup chicken stock*

Thickening:
2 *tablespoons cornstarch*
mixed with
2 *teaspoons soy sauce*
4 *tablespoons water*

Cut the beans into 1½-inch sections and parboil them in boiling water for about 3 minutes or just as they turn bright green. Drain and run through cold water. Cut the lamb against the grain into thin slices. Heat a frying pan with oil and when it is hot add salt and pepper. Add the lamb and sauté over medium heat till it is brown, stirring constantly. Now add the stock, cover, and when it comes to a boil, simmer for 5 minutes. Add the beans and leave off the cover. Add the thickening and cook for 5 minutes, stirring constantly. Serve on a platter when the sauce is thick and smooth.

❋ Sautéed Lamb

❋ CH'AO YANG JO

1½ pounds lean lamb	Marinade:
2 tablespoons oil	2 tablespoons soy sauce
	1 teaspoon salt
	1 tablespoon sherry
	2 stalks scallions

Cut the lamb against the grain into very thin slices and coat them with a mixture of soy sauce, salt and sherry. Cut the scallions into 1-inch sections and add to the liquid. Marinate the meat for 15 minutes, turning frequently.

Heat pan with the oil and when it is very hot sauté the meat for 2 minutes or until completely seared, stirring constantly. Serve immediately.

❋ Jellied Lamb

❋ YANG JO KAO

4 pounds shoulder of lamb	½ teaspoon salt
2 tablespoons sherry	3 stalks scallions
8 tablespoons soy sauce	2 cups boiling water
1 teaspoon sugar	

Cut off and discard all the fat from the meat, but be sure to keep all the bones, for this is where the gelatin will come from. Place the meat in a saucepan over high heat. Add the sherry, soy sauce, sugar and salt and bring to a boil. Cut the scallions into 1½-inch sections and add to the saucepan. Add the water slowly and when it comes to a boil, turn the heat low and simmer for 3 hours. Remove from the fire and cool. Remove all the bones and discard. Transfer the meat and liquid into a loaf pan. When it is cold skim the oil which floats on top and discard. Place the pan in the refrigerator overnight. Cut into ½-inch slices and serve cold.

Should the liquid not gel because of inadequate gelatinous stuff in the bones, melt 1 package of gelatin powder to 2 cups of hot liquid, mix well and pour over the meat. Put in the coldest part of the refrigerator and it should gel in 2 or 3 hours.

SPECIALTY MEATS

✳ *Sautéed Beef Kidney*

✳ CH'AO YAO HUA

1 *pound beef kidneys*
1½ *tablespoons cornstarch*
1½ *tablespoons water*
2½ *tablespoons sherry*

1 *onion, chopped fine*
2 *tablespoons soy sauce*
½ *teaspoon salt*
2 *tablespoons oil*

Cut the kidneys in half and carefully cut away and discard the membranes, white veins and the core. Soak the kidneys in cold water for ½ hour and wash thoroughly. Slice them as thin as possible. Blend the cornstarch with the water and add sherry, soy sauce, salt and onion. Marinate the kidneys in this mixture for 15 minutes. Heat a pan with the oil and when it is boiling hot add the kidneys and sauté for 2 or 3 minutes, stirring constantly. The kidneys should be cooked as quickly as possible and should be crisp and not chewy. Serve very hot.

✳ Sweet and Sour Pork Kidney

✳ T'ANG TS'U YAU HUA

2 pounds pork kidneys	Sauce:
2 tablespoons sherry	2 tablespoons cornstarch
2 onions	1 tablespoon soy sauce
4 tablespoons oil	4 tablespoons vinegar
½ teaspoon salt	4 tablespoons sugar
⅛ teaspoon pepper	4 tablespoons chicken stock

Wash the kidneys well and cut off and discard the membranes, the white veins and the core. Slice the kidneys as thin as possible and soak in a bowl of cold water for 1 hour, changing the water two or three times. Just before cooking, coat the kidneys with the sauce mixture and let it marinate for 1 or 2 minutes. Cut the onions into eighths. Heat a pan with 2 tablespoons of oil and when it is hot, add the onions and sauté for 1 minute. Remove the onions before they become transparent and set aside. Add the remaining oil to the pan and allow it to become boiling hot. Add the kidneys and sauté over very high heat for 20 seconds and then add the onions and sauté for another 40 seconds and turn off the heat and stir once or twice. Sprinkle with pepper and salt and serve at once.

✳ Sweet and Sour Chicken Livers

✳ T'ANG TS'U CHI KAN

8 chicken livers, cut in half	Sauce:
1 green pepper	2 tablespoons cornstarch
1 slice pineapple	mixed with
2 tablespoons oil	1 tablespoon soy sauce
½ teaspoon salt	4 tablespoons vinegar
⅛ teaspoon pepper	4 tablespoons sugar
4 tablespoons chicken stock	½ cup chicken stock

Cut the green pepper into ½-inch pieces and the pineapple into 10 chunks and set them aside. Heat a pan with the oil, salt and pepper and when it is hot add the livers and sauté for 1 minute, stirring constantly. Remove the liver from the pan and drain. Add the chicken stock to the oily pan with the peppers and pineapple. Bring to a boil, cover the pan and turn the heat down and simmer for 5 minutes. Add the livers and the blended ingredients for the sauce and cook slowly, stirring well. When the sauce thickens and becomes smooth, turn off the heat, stir a few times and serve in a shallow bowl.

✳ Deep-Fried Chicken Livers

✳ CH'AO CHI KAN

8 chicken livers, cut in half	½ cup water
3 tablespoons soy sauce	¼ teaspoon baking powder
2 tablespoons sherry	enough oil for deep frying
½ cup flour	⅛ teaspoon white pepper

Marinate the chicken livers in a mixture of soy sauce and sherry for 15 minutes. Sift the baking powder with the flour and blend with the water. Coat liver with the mixture and let it stand for a few minutes.

Heat a pan with 1 inch of oil and when it is hot add the liver and fry it for 2 minutes. Remove and drain. Place on a shallow dish and sprinkle with white pepper. Serve hot.

✳ Fried Duck Liver

✳ CH'AO YA KAN

8 duck livers, sliced	1 teaspoon cornstarch
⅛ teaspoon pepper	6 tablespoons oil
½ teaspoon salt	½ clove garlic

2 *slices ginger*
2 *stalks scallions*
1 *bamboo shoot, shredded*
4 *mushrooms*
4 *tablespoons soy sauce*
½ *teaspoon sugar*
1 *teaspoon sesame seed oil*

6 *tablespoons chicken stock*
1 *teaspoon sherry*

Thickening:
1 *teaspoon cornstarch*
mixed with
2 *tablespoons water*

Mix the pepper and salt with the cornstarch and coat the liver with it. Heat a pan with the oil and when it is very hot fry the liver for 1 minute. Remove the liver and drain it well. Add the garlic, ginger and scallion and sauté till the scallion is lightly browned. Add the bamboo shoot, mushrooms, soy sauce, sugar, sesame seed oil and chicken stock and let it simmer for 2 minutes. Return the liver to the pan and when it is hot, add the sherry and the thickening and cook till it becomes smooth and thick. Serve at once in a shallow bowl

✳ Red-Cooked Oxtail

✳ HUNG SHAO NIU WEI

3 *pounds oxtail*
4 *cups hot water*
1 *tablespoon sherry*
4 *tablespoons soy sauce*

1 *teaspoon salt*
4 *slices ginger*
1 *teaspoon sugar*

Cut the oxtail into 1-inch sections, place in a heavy saucepan and cover with the hot water. Bring to a boil, add the sherry, the soy sauce, salt and ginger and simmer for 2½ hours. Add the sugar and simmer for another ½ hour. The meat should come off easily at the touch of the chopsticks and the gravy should be thick. Serve very hot in a deep bowl.

✳ Red-Cooked Pigs' Feet

✳ HUNG SHAO CHU CHIAO

4 *pigs' feet*	1 *teaspoon salt*
2 *tablespoons soy sauce*	2 *cups hot water*
2 *tablespoons sherry*	2 *teaspoons sugar*
2 *slices ginger*	

Wash the feet well and cut each into quarters. Put in a heavy saucepan with the sherry, soy sauce, ginger and salt, turn up the heat and add the hot water slowly. When it is boiling, turn down the heat, cover and simmer for 2 hours. Add the sugar and continue cooking for another hour. When ready the meat and bones should be nearly falling apart and the gravy very thick. Serve in a deep bowl.

✳ Pigs' Feet in Sweet-Sour Sauce

✳ T'IEN SUAN CHU CHIAO

2 *pigs' feet*	4 *tablespoons soy sauce*
4 *tablespoons oil*	8 *tablespoons vinegar*
2 *slices ginger*	4 *cups water*
2 *tablespoons sherry*	8 *tablespoons sugar*

Wash the pigs' feet and chop into quarters. Dry them carefully. Heat a pan with the oil and when it is very hot add the pigs' feet and brown them well. Add the ginger, sherry and the soy sauce and stir once or twice. Add the vinegar and water and when it begins to boil, cover the pan, turn the heat low and simmer for 30 minutes, being careful that the liquid does not dry up. If it shows signs of doing so, add a mixture of water and soy sauce. Turn the pigs' feet, add sugar and simmer for another 30 minutes or until the meat and bones start to separate. Serve in a shallow bowl.

✳ Duck Tongue Soup

✳ YA SHE T'ANG

24 ducks' tongues	1 teaspoon salt
2 slices ginger	1 tablespoon sherry
1 stalk scallion, cut into	6 cups chicken stock
1-inch sections	⅛ teaspoon pepper

Place the tongues, ginger, scallion and half of the salt in a bowl. Place on a rack in a saucepan filled up to 2 inches of water and steam for 1 hour.

Bring the chicken stock to a boil and add the rest of the ingredients with the ducks' tongues. When it comes to a boil, correct the seasoning. Serve in a deep bowl.

✳ Red-Cooked Ox Tongue

✳ HUNG SHAO NIU SHEH

1 3-pound ox tongue	1 teaspoon salt
4 cups water	3 slices ginger
1 tablespoon sherry	1 teaspoon sugar
4 tablespoons soy sauce	

Put the tongue in a heavy saucepan, cover with the water and bring to a boil. Remove from the water to pull off the skin and trim the tongue. Return to the water and add the sherry, soy sauce, salt and ginger and bring to the boil again. Turn down the heat and simmer for 2 hours. Add the sugar and continue to simmer for another hour. Remove the tongue from the gravy, cut into slices, arrange in a bowl and cover with the gravy. Serve very hot.

✳ Chicken with Pork Tripe

✳ CHI JO CHU TU

1 pork tripe	2 slices ginger
1 tablespoon salt	2 stalks scallions
1 2-pound chicken	6 cups water

Wash the pork tripe well and soak in cold salty water for an hour. Remove from the water and rinse it well. Discard the water. Place the chicken in a heavy saucepan with tripe, ginger, scallions and water. Bring to a boil, lower the heat and simmer for 3 hours.

Cut the tripe into strips 2 inches by 1 inch and place in a deep bowl. Transfer the chicken with the soup carefully (as it will come apart at a touch of the chopsticks) to the bowl. Serve with side dishes of thick imported soy sauce.

✳ Red-Cooked Pork Tripe

✳ HUNG SHAO CHU TU

1 pound pork tripe	2 tablespoons soy sauce
1 tablespoon salt for cleaning tripe	½ teaspoon salt
	1 teaspoon sugar
1 cup hot water	1 onion, cut in half
1 tablespoon sherry	2 slices ginger

Wash the tripe and place in a bowl of cold water with 1 tablespoon salt; let soak for 2 hours. Remove from the water and rinse carefully. Discard the salted water. Place the tripe in a saucepan, fill with fresh water and bring to a boil. Remove, and discard the water. Cut the tripe into slices 2 inches by ½ inch and place in a pan. Add the hot water, sherry, soy sauce, salt, sugar, onion and ginger. Bring to a boil, cover the saucepan, turn down the heat and simmer for 2 hours. Serve very hot in a shallow bowl.

UNUSUAL DISHES

✱ *The Fire Pot*

✱ HUO KUO

This is not just a recipe for one dish but a meal in itself. The main feature is that the food is cooked at table in a Chinese chafing dish, which is a large brass pot with a funnel running up the center; but any chafing dish with an electric hot plate would do. All the ingredients are prepared beforehand in the kitchen and arranged on dishes around the boiling fire pot half-filled with chicken stock. The following dishes will be ample for 6 to 8 people. The meat and fish are boned and cut as thin as possible and arranged attractively, one layer deep, on plates.

 2 *plates thinly sliced chicken (about 1½ pounds)*
 2 *plates thinly sliced pork (about 1½ pounds)*

2 *plates thinly sliced beef (about 1½ pounds)*
2 *plates thinly sliced fish (sole, halibut) (about 1½ pounds)*
2 *plates thinly sliced chicken liver (1 pound)*
1 *plate pork kidneys (1 pair)*
¼ *pound pea starch vermicelli, previously boiled in water*
   for 30 minutes to soften
6 *stalks scallions, chopped into 1-inch sections*
½ *pound spinach, carefully washed and picked over*
1 *large bowl chicken stock for adding to the chafing dish at table*
½ *pound shredded cabbage*

Each diner is supplied with a rice bowl containing either 1 beaten egg or a sauce mixed to his own taste of soy sauce, sesame seed oil, chopped ginger, garlic and/or vegetable paste.

The diner may pick whatever he chooses from the numerous plates on the table and dip it in the boiling soup in front of him. As all the ingredients are thinly sliced, they will cook in a matter of seconds. He may let a few pieces stay in the pot to flavor the soup if he wishes, but as a rule he should hang on to his own piece with his chopsticks. When he removes the food he can either dip it in the beaten egg or in the sauce to cool or marinate, or eat it immediately, as he wishes.

Halfway through the meal put in the pea starch vermicelli. At the end of the meal the soup in the pot will be delicious. Soy sauce is never added to the pot, but is served in condiment dishes at table.

The accompanying staple would be pastry with sesame seed, Chinese steamed bread or onion biscuits. If these Chinese pastries are not available, hot rolls or toasted buns are good substitutes.

❋ Chafing-Dish Lamb

❋ YANG JO KUO

2 *pounds tenderloin of lamb*   ½ *teaspoon salt*
¼ *pound salted cabbage*   1½ *pounds celery cabbage*

½ pound egg noodles
¼ pound pea starch vermicelli
6 cups chicken broth

Condiment sauce:
½ cup soy sauce

½ cup vinegar
½ cup sherry
½ cup hot pepper sauce
½ cup sesame paste or
    peanut butter
1 cup chopped scallions

Cut the lamb into very thin slices and arrange on a plate. Cut the salted cabbage into small pieces, shred the celery cabbage into 1½-inch sections. Boil the noodles for about 10 minutes and drain them very dry. Boil the vermicelli for about half an hour and let soak in the hot water till it is needed. Arrange all these ingredients attractively on separate dishes and place around the chafing dish on the table. Heat the chicken broth and pour half into the chafing dish and half into a bowl on the table, for replenishing. The vegetables should be added to the chafing dish first with a few slices of meat.

Each diner should cook and hold onto his own piece of meat and not let it float around in the liquid. The egg noodles and pea starch vermicelli are added to the chafing dish halfway through the meal. Individual rice bowls should be served to each diner with enough condiment sauce to coat each slice of meat. A bowl of noodles or vermicelli will finish the meal nicely. Chinese steamed bread is an accompaniment with the meat at the beginning of the meal. Enough for 6 to 8 people.

✳ Chungking Watermelon Soup

✳ CH'UNG CH'ING HSI KUA T'ANG

1 oval watermelon about
    24 inches long
1 cup diced pork
4 cups meat of stewing
    chicken

1½ cups clams
1½ cups lobster meat
1 cup diced lamb
1 cup diced ham
1½ cups dried mushrooms

1½ cups celery, cut in shreds
1½ cups celery cabbage, cut
      in shreds
1½ cups finely chopped onions
  2 tablespoons English mustard
  1 tablespoon caraway seeds

  1 teaspoon sugar
  1 teaspoon salt
½ teaspoon pepper
  2 tablespoons soy sauce
  4 cups chicken broth
½ bunch watercress

Bring pork to a boil with enough water to cover and simmer for
½ hour. Set aside. Place all the rest of the ingredients, except the
watermelon and watercress, into a large saucepan and bring to a
boil; simmer for 2 hours. Add the cooked pork. Should the soup
be too thick, add the water in which the pork was cooked.

Cut the watermelon lengthwise, a few inches down from the
top, making an oval opening in the rind about 12 inches long.
Lift off this lid and scrape out of the melon the meat and seeds,
leaving about 1 inch of pink meat all around. (This recipe does
not require the use of the seeds or the melon meat.) Place the
watermelon in a baking pan small enough to hold the melon
steady. Add about 2 inches of water to the pan. Fill the cavity of
the melon with the soup mixture, replace the melon lid, and
bake in a hot oven (450 degrees) for about 1 hour. Add watercress, broken into pieces just before serving. Bring the melon on
a large platter to the table and serve the soup mixture and pieces
of the melon walls into individual bowls. This makes a substantial
meal for 12 people.

* Winter Melon Soup

* TUNG KUA T'ANG

  1 3½-pound chicken
  1 cup canned Chinese
      mushrooms
½ cup fresh mushrooms
  1 tablespoon diced boiled ham

  1 can lotus seeds
  5 cups chicken stock
½ teaspoon salt
⅛ teaspoon pepper
  1 6-pound winter melon

Clean chicken and remove bones. Dice very small and place in a saucepan. Dice the two types of mushrooms and add to the chicken. Add ham, lotus seeds, chicken stock, salt and pepper, and bring to a boil.

Wash the melon and cut across 2½ inches from the top. Remove all the seeds and make an even hollow in the center. Place the melon in a deep ovenproof serving bowl. Pour the soup mixture into the melon and replace the top. Place a rack in a saucepan filled up to 2 inches of boiling water and place the bowl on the rack. Cover the saucepan and steam for 3 hours. Serve the melon walls with the soup at table.

✳ Sharks' Fins

✳ YU CH'IH

2 pounds skinless sharks' fins	1 pound pork
½ pound lean pork	3 tablespoons soy sauce
½ pound fat pork	3 tablespoons sherry
1 pound beef	1 tablespoon sugar
1 leek	1 pound celery cabbage
4 stalks scallions	½ teaspoon salt
1 2-pound chicken	⅛ teaspoon pepper

Put the sharks' fins in a large saucepan with the lean and fat pork and the beef. Add enough water to cover the meat and bring to a boil. Skim from time to time. Cut the leek and scallions into 1-inch sections and add to the mixture. Simmer for 6 hours. Drain the fins and discard the soup and meat. Cut the chicken into pieces and put in a saucepan with second pound of pork and fins, cover with water and bring to a boil. Add the soy sauce, sherry and sugar and simmer for 4 or 5 hours. Cut the celery cabbage into 2-inch sections and add to the mixture and cook for 1 hour longer. By this time the fins should be very tender. Discard the chicken and pork. Season the thick sauce with salt and pepper.

Put the cabbage in a shallow bowl and pour the sharks' fins and the sauce on top; serve very hot.

✳ Turnip Patties

✳ LO PO KAO

2 cups chopped turnips	2 tablespoons chopped parsley
½ cup rice flour	½ teaspoon salt
4 slices crisp bacon	⅛ teaspoon pepper
8 fresh mushrooms, chopped fine	1 egg
4 shrimps, minced	2 tablespoons water
3 stalks scallions, chopped fine	enough oil for deep frying

Boil the turnips for about 20 minutes or until tender. Drain well and put through a blender. Combine the rice flour, bacon, mushrooms, shrimps, scallions, parsley, salt and pepper and mix with the turnips. Put in a square pan about 1 inch deep and steam for 1½ hours. Remove from the steamer and let cool. Cut loaf into 1-inch cubes and dip into the egg beaten with water. Heat a pan with 1 inch of oil and when it is very hot, fry the turnip cubes in this till it is well browned on all sides. Serve very hot as an appetizer. Will make about 25 cubes.

This may also be served sautéed with plain oil and no egg batter, or hot and fresh, without sautéeing, just as it comes from the pan.

✳ Glutinous Rice Dumplings

✳ CHUNG-TZU

Red Bean Filling:	2 tablespoons sugar
2 cups red beans	1 tablespoon lard

Boil the red beans till very soft. Hang in a 3-layer cheesecloth bag and strain. When beans are very dry, put them through a blender. Heat a pan with the lard. Sauté the paste with sugar till all the oil is used up. Set aside as filling.

Chung-Tzu:
12 rush leaves
3 cups glutinous rice

4 heaped tablespoons red bean filling
string (colored)

Soak and wash the rush leaves in hot water; cut off the hard stems. Put in a large basin and pour boiling water over them so that they will become pliable.

Wash glutinous rice, soak for 1 or 2 hours, and drain. Have red bean filling ready.

Make one leaf into a pocket by turning the stem end of the leaf downward about 6 inches from the end, toward you, and bending about a quarter of the leaf lengthwise like a paper cup. Put 2 large tablespoons rice in the hollow, one heaped tablespoon filling on top of that, and cover the whole with another two tablespoons of rice. Bend the long end of the leaf away from you and cover the filling, making a neat triangle. The fuller the package, the easier it is to fold. Now use another leaf to fold over the corners which are loose, making the corners distinct by bending the leaves neatly. Use 2 or 3 leaves depending on need. Tie up loosely with string. It is tied loosely because when the rice cooks it will expand. Drop into rapidly boiling water and boil for 3 hours. Serve with leaves.

✳ Moon Cakes

✳ YUËH PING

½ cup jujubes, quartered
½ cup green preserved plums, quartered
3 preserved cherries, quartered

2 tablespoons chopped walnut meats
2 tablespoons preserved ginger
4 tablespoons pine nuts

½ cup brown sugar
¼ cup red wine
1 cup chopped boiled beef
¼ cup chopped suet

6 lotus seeds
½ teaspoon powdered ginger
¼ teaspoon salt

Pie crust

Mix all the ingredients together in a saucepan and cook slowly for 1 hour, stirring frequently. Cool before using.

Roll out the pie crust very thin and line small tart pans with it. Fill the pans ¾ full with the mixture and cover with a top of crust. With the remainder of the pastry, cut out crescents and other shapes denoting the moon (rabbits, etc.) and put on top of the crust. Preheat the oven to 475 degrees and bake tarts for 20 to 30 minutes. Serve hot or cold on the fifteenth day of the eighth moon (Harvest Moon).

EGG
DISHES

✳ Egg Pockets

✳ CHI TAN CHIAO

1 *tablespoon oil*

Filling:
½ *pound ground pork*
1 *teaspoon sesame seed oil*
1 *stalk scallion, finely chopped*
½ *teaspoon soy sauce*
¼ *teaspoon sugar*
½ *teaspoon salt*

Egg mixture:
4 *eggs*
1 *teaspoon salt*
⅛ *teaspoon pepper*
2 *tablespoons oil*

Heat a pan with 1 tablespoon oil and sauté the meat for 1 minute. Add the rest of the filling mixture and stir for 2 minutes. Set it aside and let it cool.

Beat the eggs till they are very light and season with salt and pepper. Heat a pan and add only enough oil to grease the pan. Pour in enough egg to make a very thin round pancake 3 inches in diameter. Place a tablespoon of meat filling on half of the pancake and fold over the other half to cover the meat; press down the edge so that it will seal. Turn onto the other side with a spatula and cook for ½ minute. Remove to a warm plate. Oil the pan again and continue to make these little pockets, keeping them warm till the egg is used up. Will make about 8. Serve hot.

✳ Savory Egg Custard

✳ CHEN CHI TAN

3 eggs	2 stalks scallions
½ teaspoon salt	½ teaspoon soy sauce
½ cup chicken broth	

Beat the eggs well, add salt and broth and put in an ovenproof serving bowl. Chop the scallions up fine and sprinkle on top of the eggs. Place a rack in a pan and fill up to 2 inches of water. Place the bowl on the rack and steam for 15 minutes or until custard is firm. Before serving add a few drops of soy sauce to the custard. Serve very hot.

✳ Steamed Eggs with Minced Pork

✳ CHI TAN CHEN JO MI

4 eggs, well beaten	Garnish:
½ pound minced pork	1 teaspoon soy sauce
1 stalk scallion, chopped fine	1 ounce minced ham
1 teaspoon salt	1 stalk scallion, chopped fine
1 teaspoon oil	
½ cup chicken stock	

Mix together the eggs, pork, scallion, salt, oil and chicken stock. Pour all into ovenproof bowl. Place a rack in a large saucepan and fill up to 2 inches of boiling water. Place the bowl on the rack and cover. Steam for 15 to 20 minutes or until the egg is set. Remove from the saucepan, sprinkle with the garnish and serve immediately in the hot bowl.

❋ Steamed Eggs with Oysters

❋ CHI TAN CHEN LI HUANG

10 oysters, minced fine	1 teaspoon soy sauce
2 ounces fat pork, minced fine	1 teaspoon oil
2 Spanish olives, chopped fine	1 teaspoon salt
1 stalk scallion, chopped fine	⅛ teaspoon pepper
4 eggs, well beaten	2 tablespoons water

Mix all the ingredients thoroughly together and pour into an ovenproof serving bowl. Place a rack in a deep saucepan and fill up to 2 inches of boiling water. Place the bowl on the rack, cover and steam for 10 minutes or until the eggs are set. Serve in the hot bowl.

❋ Salted Eggs with Steamed Pork

❋ HSIEN TAN CHEN JO

1 pound ground pork	½ teaspoon sugar
2 water chestnuts	4 tablespoons water
2 salted eggs	⅛ teaspoon pepper
1 teaspoon cornstarch	1 teaspoon soy sauce
½ teaspoon salt	1 tablespoon oil

Peel and chop fine the water chestnuts and set aside. Separate the egg whites from the yolks and mix the whites well with the rest of the ingredients. Place the meat in an ovenproof serving bowl and gently place the two egg yolks on top of the meat. Place a rack in a large saucepan filled up to 2 inches of boiling water. Place the bowl on the rack and cover. Steam for about 20 minutes or until the meat is well cooked. Serve hot.

✳ Steamed Eggs with Shrimps

✳ CHI TAN CHEN HSIA

½ pound shrimps, shelled
    and deveined
¼ pound pork, minced
4 stalks scallions, chopped
    fine
1½ teaspoons salt

6 eggs
½ cup water

Garnish:
1 stalk scallion, chopped fine
1 teaspoon soy sauce

Chop the shrimps, add to the meat, mix well together and chop fine. Add salt and scallions and mix thoroughly with the meat mixture till it is quite smooth. Meanwhile, beat the eggs with ½ cup water until frothy. Place the meat in the bottom of a deep ovenproof bowl and pour the eggs over the meat.

Place a rack in a large saucepan and fill up to 2 inches of water. Place the bowl on the rack and steam for 30 minutes, or until the meat is thoroughly cooked. Remove from the steamer and sprinkle the garnish on top. Serve very hot.

✳ Imperial Eggs

✳ LIU HUANG TS'AI

6 egg yolks
2 cups chicken stock
1 tablespoon sherry
1 teaspoon salt
½ cup chopped water chestnuts

4 slices Smithfield ham,
    chopped fine
2 tablespoons cornstarch
4 tablespoons water
4 tablespoons oil

Beat the egg yolks and add slowly to the stock. Add the sherry, salt, water chestnuts and half the ham and beat well. Mix the cornstarch with the water and add to the egg mixture. Stir vigorously.

Heat a pan with the oil and when it boils, pour in the egg mixture and stir constantly till it becomes thick and smooth. Pour into a shallow bowl and sprinkle with the remaining chopped ham. Serve immediately.

✳ Sharks' Fins Omelet

✳ YU CH'IH CH'AO CHI TAN

½ cup shredded sharks' fins
2 tablespoons oil
1 slice ginger
2 stalks scallions, cut into
   1-inch sections
2 tablespoons sherry

1 cup chicken stock
6 eggs, well beaten
1 teaspoon salt, pepper to
   taste
6 tablespoons oil

Soak the sharks' fins in boiling water for 4 hours. Drain in a colander, run cold water over and soak in cold water for 2 more hours. Wash and drain again. Place the fins in 2 cups of water and bring to a boil, turn the heat low and simmer for ½ hour. Remove the fins from the water and drain well.

Heat a pan with the oil and when it is hot add the ginger and scallions and stir once or twice. Add the sherry, stock, sharks' fins, pepper and salt. Bring to a boil and cook slowly for 3 minutes. Drain the sharks' fins and discard ginger and scallions. Add the fins to the beaten eggs and season with salt. Reheat the pan and add 6 tablespoons oil. Pour the egg mixture into the pan and fold over slowly, being sure to leave the inside soft and semi-liquid. Remove carefully onto a flat plate with a pancake turner. Serve immediately.

✳ Shrimp Omelet

✳ CH'AO HSIA TAN

½ pound shrimps, shelled and deveined
1 tablespoon oil for shrimps
2 tablespoons soy sauce
¼ cup shredded celery
¼ cup shredded onion
3 tablespoons oil for eggs
6 eggs
½ cup water
1 teaspoon salt

Cut the shrimps into ½-inch pieces. Heat pan with 1 tablespoon oil and when it is hot add the shrimps and sauté for 1 minute. Add the soy sauce and stir once or twice. Add the celery and onion and sauté for another minute, stirring constantly. Remove from the pan and set aside.

Beat the eggs, add the water and salt and mix well together. Heat the pan with 3 tablespoons oil and pour the eggs in slowly. Form into a pancake and place the shrimps and vegetables on it. Fold over one edge and then the other and cook 2 minutes. Turn with a spatula and cook the other side for 1 minute and serve very hot on a shallow dish.

✳ Eggs Foo Yong

✳ FU JUNG TAN

1 cup crab meat
1 cup pea sprouts
4 tablespoons oil
6 eggs
6 tablespoons water
1 teaspoon salt
⅛ teaspoon pepper

Pick over the crab meat and discard foreign matter. Wash and drain the pea sprouts. Heat a pan with the oil and add the crab meat, pea sprouts, salt and pepper and sauté for 10 minutes. Beat the eggs, add water, stir well and pour into the same pan. Brown on one side, slide the egg mixture out onto a plate, turn the other side onto the pan and brown. Serve very hot on a flat dish.

✳ Preserved Eggs

✳ P'I TAN

12 *eggs*	6 *cups lime*
2 *cups mud*	4 *cups rice husks*

Mix the mud with the lime and quickly cover the eggs with this mixture, then roll in rice husks so that they can be handled. Place in a cool, dark place for about 100 days, when they should be cured. Crack the lime covering and shell the eggs. Wash them with water and cut into quarters lengthwise. The white of the egg will have become dark green and gelatinous and the yolk orange-green; and the taste will be reminiscent of cheese.

Serve with imported table soy sauce as an hors d'oeuvre or as an accompaniment for congee.

✳ Salted Eggs

✳ HSIEN TAN

12 *chicken or duck eggs*	8 *cups water*
1 *cup coarse salt*	

Boil the water with the salt and let it cool. Place the eggs in a wide-necked jar and cover with the salted water. Let stand at warm room temperature for about 4 weeks.

To serve the eggs, boil for about 20 minutes or until they are hard-boiled. Shell them and cut into quarters lengthwise. The yolks will be very red and the whites quite salty. Serve with congee.

✳ Tea Eggs

✳ CH'A TAN

8 eggs	1 tablespoon salt
4 cups water	1 tangerine rind
2 teaspoons black tea leaves	

Place the eggs in a saucepan, cover with water, bring to a boil and simmer for 1 hour. Remove from the hot water and plunge into cold water for ½ minute to cool. Crack but do not remove the shells.

Bring the water in the saucepan to a boil again and add the tea leaves, salt and tangerine rind. Lower the eggs into this mixture and simmer for another 2 hours. Turn off the heat and let the eggs stand in the liquid for ½ hour. Shell the eggs and cut into quarters lengthwise. The yolks should be soft again because of the long cooking time.

✳ Braised Pigeon Eggs

✳ HUNG SHAO KO TAN

4 pigeon eggs	Sauce:
1 bamboo shoot, sliced	2 tablespoons soy sauce
2 mushrooms, sliced	½ teaspoon sugar
½ cup water	1 tablespoon sherry
¼ cup flour	1 teaspoon cornstarch
1 cup oil	

Boil the eggs for 5 minutes, remove from the pan and run them under cold water. When cold, shell them. Boil the bamboo shoot and mushrooms in water for 5 minutes; remove and set aside. Soak cooked eggs in the sauce mixture for a few minutes and then roll in the flour. Heat a pan with the oil and when it is very hot fry the eggs until they are brown, then remove and drain.

Pour away the oil except for 3 tablespoons of it and reheat the pan. Add bamboo shoots, mushrooms and sauce mixture and heat. Add the eggs and simmer for 10 seconds. Serve very hot in a shallow dish.

❉ Pigeon Eggs in Tomatoes

❉ HSI HUNG SHIH KO TAN

4 pigeon eggs	2 tablespoons soy sauce
¼ cup tomato juice	½ cup sherry
2 tablespoons flour	2 tablespoons finely chopped
½ tablespoon ground ginger	onion
½ teaspoon salt	½ cup toasted bread crumbs
⅛ teaspoon pepper	½ cup crumbled corn flakes

Boil the eggs for 15 minutes, shell them and set them aside. They will look gelatinous.

Mix together in a saucepan the tomato juice, flour, ginger, salt, pepper, soy sauce, sherry and onion. Bring the ingredients to a boil, stirring constantly. Arrange the eggs in a small baking pan and pour sauce over them. Sprinkle with bread crumbs and corn-flakes and bake in a hot oven at 450 degrees for about 5 minutes. Serve very hot.

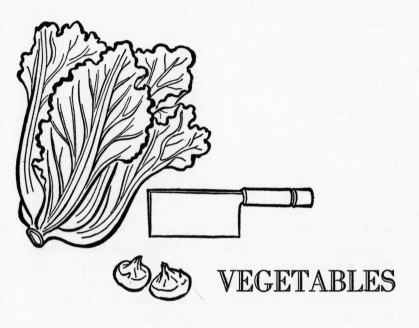

VEGETABLES

✳ Sautéed Chinese Broccoli

✳ CH'AO KAI LAN TS'AI

2 pounds Chinese broccoli
2 scallions
3 tablespoons oil

½ teaspoon salt
½ teaspoon sugar
1 teaspoon soy sauce

Cut the broccoli into 1½-inch lengths and the scallions into 1-inch sections. Heat a pan with oil and when it is hot add the scallions and sauté for ½ minute. Increase the heat, add the broccoli and stir constantly till it turns jade green. Add the salt, sugar and soy sauce and stir once or twice. Serve very hot in a shallow dish.

✳ Chinese Cabbage Hearts with Crab-Meat Sauce

✳ HSIEH YU CH'AO PAI TS'AI

½ pound crab meat
1 pound Chinese cabbage
½ teaspoon baking soda
2 tablespoons oil
⅛ teaspoon pepper
½ teaspoon salt
boiling water

Sauce:
2 tablespoons oil
1 teaspoon sherry
1 cup chicken stock
⅛ teaspoon pepper
½ teaspoon salt

Thickening:
1 tablespoon cornstarch
mixed with
½ cup water

Wash the cabbage hearts and cut into quarters. Plunge them into a saucepan of hot water mixed with baking soda for 1 minute. Drain well. Heat pan with 2 tablespoons oil and sauté the vegetable till it is well cooked and soft. Season with salt and pepper. Place on serving platter and keep hot in the oven or on a hot plate. Reheat the pan with 2 tablespoons oil and sauté the crab meat for 1 minute. Add the sherry and chicken stock and season with pepper and salt. Add the thickening to the crab and continue to stir for 1 minute. When it is very hot and the sauce well thickened, pour over vegetables and serve immediately.

✳ Braised Cabbage with Mushrooms

✳ TUNG KU CH'AO PAI TS'AI

2 tablespoons oil
3 tablespoons dried shrimps
1 pound celery cabbage
2 cups water
½ teaspoon salt

2 tablespoons soy sauce
1 teaspoon sugar
4 mushrooms, soaked and
    sliced
1 red pepper, sliced

Heat a pan with oil and sauté dried shrimps for 2 minutes. Cut the cabbage into quarters and then into 2-inch sections. Boil 2 cups water, add the cabbage and cook for 10 minutes. Remove the cabbage and drain. When it is dry add to the shrimps, sauté together for 4 minutes and then add the salt. Add the cabbage water to the vegetable, bring to a boil, turn down the heat and simmer for 10 minutes. Add the soy sauce, sugar, mushrooms and red pepper and simmer for another 10 minutes. Serve very hot in a shallow bowl.

✳ Creamed Chinese Cabbage

✳ NAI YU PAI TS'AI

1½ pounds celery cabbage
½ scant cup chicken fat
¾ teaspoon salt
4 tablespoons minced ham
⅛ teaspoon pepper

Thickening:
1 cup milk
mixed with
2 tablespoons cornstarch
1 teaspoon monosodium glutamate

Wash the celery cabbage well and cut lengthwise ¼ inch wide, then into 2½-inch sections. Heat pan with chicken fat and when it is very hot add the cabbage. Turn down the heat to medium and cover for 10 minutes or till vegetable is tender, stirring occasionally. Season with salt. Prepare thickening, stir into the vegetable and cook for about 4 minutes or till the liquid thickens. Be sure that the starchy taste is gone. It is better to overcook than to undercook this dish.

Turn into a deep round platter, sprinkle with ham and a dash of pepper and serve immediately.

✳ Cauliflower, Water Chestnuts and Mushrooms

✳ TUNG KU CH'AO TS'AI HUA

1 small cauliflower	½ cup soup stock
2 tablespoons oil	1 teaspoon sherry
5 mushrooms, soaked	2 tablespoons soy sauce
4 water chestnuts	2 tablespoons cornstarch
½ cup mushroom water	1 teaspoon oil

Cut the cauliflower into florets, pour boiling water over them and
let them stand in the water for 5 minutes. Remove from the
water, drain and set aside. Heat a pan with the oil and when it
is hot add the mushrooms and sauté for ½ minute, add the
water chestnuts, mushroom water, soup stock, sherry, soy sauce,
cornstarch and oil. Bring to a boil and then turn down the heat;
simmer for ½ minute, stirring constantly. Add cauliflower and
cook another minute, stirring well. When it is very hot turn out
onto a shallow dish and serve immediately.

✳ Celery Cabbage with Chestnuts

✳ LI TZU CH'AO PAI TS'AI

½ pound chestnuts	boiling water
1 pound celery cabbage	½ teaspoon monosodium
1 tablespoon oil	glutamate
1 cup chicken stock	
1 tablespoon dried scallops,	Thickening:
soaked	½ teaspoon cornstarch
1 teaspoon salt	mixed with
½ teaspoon baking soda	2 tablespoons water

Shell and blanch the chestnuts and set aside. Wash and quarter
the cabbage and cut into 2-inch sections. Plunge into a saucepan
of boiling water mixed with ½ teaspoon soda for 1 minute. Drain

well. Heat pan with oil and when hot sauté the cabbage over high heat for 2 minutes. Add stock, scallops, chestnuts, salt, monosodium glutamate and bring to a boil. Lower the heat and let it simmer for 20 minutes or until the chestnuts are soft. Add the thickening and when the gravy becomes smooth and thick, turn into a deep bowl and serve very hot.

✳ Celery with Mushrooms

✳ TUNG KU CH'AO CH'IN TS'AI

1 bunch celery	2 tablespoons soy sauce
¼ pound fresh mushrooms	1 teaspoon salt
2 tablespoons oil	1 teaspoon sugar

Wash celery and cut the stalks, with the rolling cut, into 1-inch pieces. Heat a pan with oil and when it is hot sauté the mushrooms for 1 minute. Add the soy sauce, salt and sugar. Stir two or three times, then add the celery and sauté for 3 minutes, stirring constantly. Serve very hot in a shallow dish.

✳ Cucumber Salad

✳ LIANG PAN HUANG KUA

1 medium cucumber	1 tablespoon sugar
2 tablespoons vinegar	1 teaspoon chopped ginger
3 tablespoons soy sauce	2 tablespoons sesame seed oil

Slice the cucumber very thin and add the vinegar, soy sauce, sugar and ginger. Allow it to marinate for a few hours in the refrigerator and then add the sesame seed oil. Serve very cold in a shallow dish.

* Pickled Radish

* CHIANG LO PO

1 bunch radishes   1 tablespoon sugar
3 tablespoons vinegar   2 tablespoons sesame seed oil
3 tablespoons soy sauce

Cut off tops of radishes; wash then crush radishes with the blade of a chopper. Add vinegar, soy sauce and sugar. Put in the refrigerator and let marinate for a few hours. Add the sesame seed oil and serve in a shallow bowl.

* Mushrooms and Snow Peas in Oyster Sauce

* HAO YU TUNG KU CH'AO HSUËH TOU

6 ounces dried mushrooms   Thickening:
4 stalks scallions   1 teaspoon cornstarch
1 piece ginger   2 tablespoons water
½ teaspoon soy sauce
½ teaspoon salt   4 tablespoons oyster sauce
1 teaspoon sugar   ½ pound snow peas
1 teaspoon cornstarch   2 tablespoons oil
2 tablespoons oil   1 teaspoon salt
1½ cups chicken broth
½ cup mushroom water

Wash mushrooms and soak in a small bowl of boiling water for about ½ hour. Remove from liquid and cut off stems; set the liquid aside. Cut the scallions into 1-inch lengths and shred the ginger. Mix together in a large bowl the soy sauce, salt, sugar, cornstarch and mushrooms. Be sure that the mushrooms are well coated with the liquid mixture. Heat pan with the oil and when it is very hot brown the mushrooms. Add scallions and the ginger and sauté together for 5 minutes. Add the chicken broth and ½ cup mushroom water and simmer for 10 minutes. Add the thickening and simmer for another 2 minutes and add oyster sauce.

Wash and stem the snow peas, leaving the pods intact. Plunge them into a saucepan of boiling water for 60 seconds. Drain well. Heat pan with the oil and when it is very hot sauté the snow peas with salt for 1 minute. Remove from the heat and drain the peas well. Place on a shallow platter and cover with the very hot mushroom mixture.

✳ Vegetable Chop Suey

✳ SU CHA SUI

2 tablespoons oil
¼ cup sliced pork
¼ cup sliced celery
½ cup sliced celery cabbage
¼ cup sliced onion
½ cup bean sprouts
½ cup chicken stock
½ teaspoon salt
⅛ teaspoon pepper

½ teaspoon monosodium glutamate
½ teaspoon soy sauce

Thickening:
2 teaspoons cornstarch mixed with
4 tablespoons water

Heat a pan with oil and when it is hot add the pork and sauté for about 20 seconds. Add the celery, cabbage, onion and bean sprouts and continue to sauté for 2 more minutes. Add the stock, salt, pepper and monosodium glutamate. When it boils, cover, turn down the heat and allow it to simmer for about 4 minutes. Add the soy sauce and thickening and stir. When the sauce becomes smooth and thick, turn out onto a shallow platter and serve immediately.

✳ Baked Water Chestnuts

✳ K'AO PI CHI

1 *pound water chestnuts*	2 *teaspoons oil*
6 *eggs*	1 *teaspoon salt*
1 *cup milk*	⅛ *teaspoon pepper*

Peel water chestnuts and wash well. Cut into ¼-inch cubes. Separate the eggs and beat the whites till they are light and fluffy. Set aside. Mix the yolks with the milk and oil and season with the pepper and salt. Place the cubed chestnuts in a baking dish and mix well with the yolk mixture. Cover with the egg whites. Preheat the oven to 375 degrees and bake for ½ hour. Serve very hot.

SOY BEANS
AND BEAN CURD

✳ The Story of the Soy Bean

This miracle bean is a legume belonging to the same family as the navy bean and has been known to the Chinese for centuries. Legend has it that the Emperor Chen-nun wrote a treatise on it in the year 2800 B.C.

This bean, besides being rich in body-building protein and minerals, is pleasing to the palate. For years the Chinese prepared the bean in its natural state in their cuisine. However, 2,000 years ago they discovered accidentally how to grow bean sprouts, and since that date, derivatives of the bean have been more popular. The story of the discovery of the bean sprout is interesting enough to be told here.

A party of explorers sailed up the Yangtze in a flat-bottomed boat to seek the source of the river. They expected to be away for quite some time and had, therefore, prepared a large supply of provisions to take with them. They did not know, however, that there were rapids in the upper Yangtze, and the journey took much longer than expected. They encountered bad weather, a good part of their provisions was spoiled by dampness and their supplies ran short. During the last few days they were reduced to a few sacks of dried beans in the bottom of the boat. When they finally opened the bags they found the beans sprouting. Having nothing else to sustain them, the explorers ventured to eat the sprouts and found them good. Upon returning to the coast they told the world of their discovery.

From the simple bean, the ingenious Chinese learned how to make the bean milk, and from the milk the curds, and from the curds the cheese, in the same way Westerners had developed cheeses and other products of cow's milk. The soy bean is so nutritious that it is known as the cow of China.

✳ To Sprout the Soy Bean

Mung beans are used to grow bean sprouts. They must be of the young, small, black variety, because if they are more than one year old they will not sprout. Chlorinated lime will prevent mold growth, so it is necessary to have some on hand for better results.

Wash the beans and pick them over. Soak them overnight in lukewarm water with chlorinated lime. The next morning put them in a crock that is large enough to let the quantity swell four times and that has a hole at the bottom for draining—or in a colander lined with cotton cloth. Keep the beans dark and moist in about 75-degree temperature. Cover the crock or the colander with a dark cloth to exclude the light. Water the beans slowly every two hours, being sure that the water runs through the holes and is well drained. At night add a pinch of chlorinated lime to the sprinkling water. The beans will be edible but not at their greatest growth in from three to five days; however, if the room is very warm they should be ready in two days. In six or eight days the sprouts will be about 3 inches long, the beans four times in bulk, so that 1 pound of beans will yield about 5 pounds of sprouts.

Soy bean sprouts may be quick-frozen. Pass through boiling water for 1 or 2 minutes. Remove them from the water, drain well and freeze.

✳ Roasted Soy Bean Nuts

✳ TS'AN TOU

1 cup dried soy beans	4 tablespoons oil
3 cups water	2 tablespoons salt, or to taste

Wash the soy beans, place them in a large bowl, cover with water and soak overnight. Remove from the water, rub with a cloth and spread out on a tray to dry. When the skin of the beans is dry, spread on a baking pan, sprinkle with oil and shake in order to coat the beans evenly. Preheat the oven to 350 degrees and place the pan on the middle shelf. Roast the beans till brown, turning and shaking the beans frequently. Sprinkle with salt and serve as a tidbit.

✳ Beef with Bean Sprouts

✳ TOU YA NIU JO

1 pound flank steak	1 teaspoon salt
2 cups bean sprouts	⅛ teaspoon pepper
2 stalks scallions	
1 tablespoon oil	Thickening:
½ clove garlic, crushed	3 tablespoons cornstarch
1 slice ginger	mixed with
	¼ cup cold water

Cut the steak against the grain into very thin pieces about 1 inch square. Wash the bean sprouts and pick them over well. Cut the scallions into 1-inch sections. Heat a pan with the oil and add the garlic, ginger, salt and pepper. When the garlic turns golden brown, remove and discard it. Sauté the meat for 1 minute and then add the bean sprouts and continue to sauté for 1 minute more, stirring constantly. Pour the thickening over the meat and when the sauce is smooth and thick, sprinkle with the scallions and serve very hot.

✳ Bean Sprouts and Celery

✳ TOU YA CH'IN TS'AI

1 pound bean sprouts	1 slice ginger, shredded
4 stalks celery	2 teaspoons soy sauce
½ onion	1 tablespoon water
3 tablespoons oil	1 pinch monosodium glutamate
½ teaspoon salt	

Wash and trim the bean sprouts. Cut the celery into 1-inch diagonal pieces and the onion into shreds. Heat a pan with the oil and when it is very hot add the sprouts, celery and onion. Sauté for about 5 minutes, stirring constantly. Add salt, ginger, soy sauce, water and monosodium glutamate. Simmer for 5 minutes and then remove from pan and serve very hot.

✳ Bean Sprouts and Pork

✳ TOU YA JO SSU

¼ pound pork, sliced	1½ tablespoons oil
	2 cups bean sprouts
Sauce:	1½ tablespoons oil for sprouts
1 tablespoon soy sauce	½ teaspoon salt
1 teaspoon sherry	
½ teaspoon cornstarch	
¼ teaspoon soy sauce	
¼ teaspoon salt	

Marinate the pork in the sauce mixture for about 15 minutes. Heat a pan with 1½ tablespoons oil and when it is hot, add the bean sprouts and sauté for 2 minutes, stirring constantly. Remove and set aside. Reheat the pan with 1½ tablespoons oil and when it is very hot add the marinated pork and sauté for 2 minutes, stirring constantly. Add the bean sprouts, and stir once or twice and add the salt. Stir again two or three times and then turn onto a shallow dish and serve immediately.

✳ Soy Bean Milk

✳ TO FU CHIANG

1 pound soy beans	½ teaspoon salt
enough water to cover beans	1 teaspoon sugar
3 quarts water	

Wash the soy beans and soak overnight in enough water to cover. Drain and discard the water; remove the skins from the beans. Grind the beans very fine, and put in a cheesecloth bag. Heat 3 quarts water to lukewarm and place the bag in it. Squeeze the ground beans through the bag till only the pulp remains. Wring the bag till it becomes very dry. Put the pan on an asbestos pad and bring the milk to a boil; simmer for 30 minutes, stirring constantly. Add sugar and salt and cool. Serve either hot or cold.

✳ Soy Bean Curd

✳ TOU FU

2 quarts soy bean milk	1 large pan of cold water
1 cup vinegar	1 teaspoon salt

Heat the bean milk to a temperature of 180 degrees and add the vinegar. Mix well and let stand for 15 minutes. Put the curd in a cheesecloth bag and dip the bag in cold water to wash away the acid. Drain the bag in a sieve for about 1 hour and squeeze out the remaining liquid. Turn the curd into a bowl and season with salt. Pack into dampened ice tray and place in a cool place until it sets. Cut into shape desired.

✳ Fried Bean Curd

✳ CHA TOU FU

4 squares bean curd   1 teaspoon salt
enough oil for deep frying

Wash the bean curds, cut them into quarters and set them aside to drain. Heat a pan and fill up to 1 inch of oil and add the salt. When it is very hot, deep-fry the curds on one side till they become golden brown, and then fry on the other side. Remove and drain the oil. The bean curds are now ready to be cooked with other ingredients.

✳ Bean Curd Cheese

✳ FU JU

4 squares bean curd   1 cup sherry
4 cups water   1 teaspoon salt
2 tablespoons salt

Cut the bean curds into 1x1x½-inch pieces and soak in water and salt for 2 days. Remove from the water and when curds are well drained, place in the sun for 2 days to dry. Arrange carefully in a deep bowl and set aside. Place a rack in a deep saucepan filled up to 2 inches of water; place the bowl on the rack and steam for 20 minutes. Remove the curds carefully to a bottle, fill with sherry and salt and cover tightly. Let the bottle stand in the sun another day, and then let it mature at room temperature from 3 to 6 months, the longer the better.

✳ Stuffed Bean Curd

✳ TOU FU CHEN JO

Filling:
½ pound minced pork
1 stalk scallion, chopped fine
1 teaspoon soy sauce
1 teaspoon sherry
1 teaspoon sesame seed oil

3 squares bean curd
1 teaspoon soy sauce
½ teaspoon sesame seed oil

Mix the ingredients for the filling well together and let stand for a few minutes.

Cut each square of bean curd into 2 triangles. Scoop a hole in the cut side and fill with the meat mixture. Place them in an ovenproof serving bowl and sprinkle with 1 teaspoon soy sauce and ½ teaspoon sesame seed oil. Place a rack in a large saucepan filled up to 2 inches of boiling water. Place the bowl on the rack, cover and steam for ½ hour. Serve hot in the bowl.

✳ Bean Curd with Sea Bass

✳ TOU FU LU YÜ

1 pound sea bass
2 tablespoons vegetable paste (Hoisin)
2 slices ginger, shredded
1 stalk scallion, chopped fine
½ teaspoon salt
⅛ teaspoon pepper

¼ teaspoon sugar
⅛ teaspoon monosodium glutamate
½ teaspoon soy sauce
2 tablespoons oil
2 squares bean curd, cut into quarters

Coat the fish with the vegetable paste and place it in an oven-proof serving bowl. Cover with ginger, scallion, salt, pepper, sugar, monosodium glutamate, soy sauce and oil. Surround the fish with bean curds. Place a rack in a large saucepan with 2 inches of water and boil rapidly. Place the bowl in the saucepan and cover. Steam the fish over high heat for 12 minutes. Serve very hot.

✳ Bean Curd with Flounder

✳ PIEN YÜ TOU FU

2 squares bean curd	1 tablespoon soy sauce
2 tablespoons oil	1 stalk scallion, cut into
1 pound flounder filet	1-inch sections
2 tablespoons sherry	½ cup water
1 slice ginger, chopped fine	salt to taste

Cut the bean curds into ½-inch cubes and set them aside. Heat a pan with the oil and when it is very hot, turn down the heat and brown the fish 2 minutes on one side and 1 minute on the other. Pour the sherry slowly over the fish and add the ginger, soy sauce, scallions, water and a little salt. Simmer for 15 minutes; then add the bean curds and cook another 5 to 7 minutes or until the fish is done. Serve in a shallow bowl immediately.

✳ Stewed Bean Curd

✳ HUNG SHAO TOU FU

5 squares bean curd	1 teaspoon salt
6 cups water	2 stalks scallions, cut into
1 pound pork, sliced thin	1-inch sections
4 tablespoons soy sauce	1 teaspoon sugar
1 package frozen peas	2 cups chicken broth
½ pound mushrooms, cut into slices	

Slice the bean curds across and then quarter the slices. Put in a saucepan and add enough water to cover the bean curds. Bring to a fast boil and continue to boil for ½ hour. Pour through a fine sieve and drain the curds. Return them to the saucepan and add all the other ingredients. Turn the heat high and bring to a boil. Cover, lower the heat and simmer for 10 minutes. Serve in a deep bowl.

✳ Braised Pork with Bean Curd

✳ TOU FU CH'AO JO

1 *pound pork*	½ *cup bean curd*
2 *cups water*	4 *tablespoons soy sauce*
3 *tablespoons oil*	½ *teaspoon salt*
1 *onion, sliced*	1 *tablespoon sugar*
1 *clove garlic*	1½ *cups chicken stock*

Put 2 cups of water with the pork in a pan and bring it to a boil; continue to cook for 4 minutes. Remove the pork and allow it to cool. Heat a pan with the oil and when it is hot add the onions and the garlic and stir till they are golden in color. Add the pork and brown on both sides. Add the bean curd, stir for one minute, then add the soy sauce, salt, sugar, and the chicken stock. Lower the heat, cover and simmer for ½ hour or until the meat is tender. Serve very hot in a shallow bowl.

✳ Bean Curd with Braised Pork

✳ TOU FU HUNG SHAO JO

1 *pound pork cut into*	1 *tablespoon brown sugar*
1½-*inch cubes*	3 *squares bean curd*
1½ *cups beef stock*	
1 *tablespoon sherry*	*Thickening:*
4 *tablespoons soy sauce*	1 *teaspoon cornstarch*
1 *cup sliced onion*	*mixed with*
1 *slice ginger, shredded*	2 *tablespoons water*
1 *clove garlic, crushed*	

Place the pork in a saucepan with the beef stock, sherry, soy sauce, onion, ginger, garlic and brown sugar. Bring to a boil, cover and turn the heat low; simmer for 15 minutes. Cut the bean curds into quarters and carefully add to the saucepan; cover and simmer for another 20 minutes. Add the thickening and continue to simmer until it is smooth and thick, stirring constantly. Serve very hot in a shallow dish.

✳ Bean Curd with Shrimps

✳ HSIA JEN TOU FU

4 *squares bean curd*	2½ *tablespoons soy sauce*
4 *tablespoons chopped,*	1½ *teaspoons sesame seed oil*
cooked shrimps	

Cut bean curds into ½-inch slices, place in a sieve and dip into boiling water for 2 or 3 seconds. Drain them well and chill. Arrange on a serving dish. Mix the shrimps with the soy sauce and sesame seed oil and serve over the bean curds. Serve chilled.

✳ Bean Curd with Scallions

✳ TS'UNG CH'AO TOU FU

5 *squares bean curd, cut*	1 *bunch scallions, cut into*
into quarters	*1-inch sections*
4 *tablespoons oil*	2 *tablespoons soy sauce*
	1½ *teaspoons salt*

Heat a pan with the oil, and when it is very hot add the scallions and sauté for 1 minute. Add the bean curds and continue to sauté for another 2 minutes. Mix the salt with the soy sauce, pour into the pan and continue to stir gently over high heat for another minute. Serve boiling hot on a platter.

✳ Bean Curd with Mushrooms

✳ TUNG KU TOU FU

½ pound fresh mushrooms, cut
    into ½-inch slices
5 squares bean curd, cut
    into ½-inch slices
4 tablespoons oil
2 tablespoons oyster sauce

Thickening:
1 tablespoon cornstarch
mixed with
3 . tablespoons cold water

Heat a pan with the oil and when it is hot add the mushrooms
and sauté for 1 minute. Carefully add the bean curds and oyster
sauce and continue to cook for 3 minutes, shaking the pan and
being careful not to break the curds. Add the thickening and continue to cook till the sauce becomes smooth and thick. When it
is very hot, serve in a shallow dish immediately.

✳ Bean Curd with Eggs

✳ TOU FU CHI TAN

4 eggs, well beaten
2 teaspoons salt
2 tablespoons cornstarch
4 tablespoons cold water

½ teaspoon monosodium
    glutamate
5 squares bean curd
4 tablespoons oil

Place the beaten eggs in a deep bowl and add the salt, cornstarch, cold water and the monosodium glutamate; mix thoroughly.
Heat a pan with 2 tablespoons oil and keep it hot. Cut the curds
into 1½-inch squares, ¼ inch thick, and dip into the egg mixture;
sauté for 2 minutes. If the pan becomes too dry add more oil.
Serve very hot on a platter.

✳ Bean Curd Soup

✳ TOU FU T'ANG

½ pound pork, sliced
3 squares bean curd
6 cups boiling water
½ teaspoon salt
1 teaspoon soy sauce

Marinade:
½ tablespoon cornstarch
1 tablespoon soy sauce
½ tablespoon sherry

Coat the meat with the marinating mixture and let it stand for a few minutes.

Cut the bean curds into ½-inch cubes and put in a pan with the boiling water; boil for 2 minutes. Add the salt, soy sauce and the seasoned meat and continue to boil for 2 minutes more. Pour into a large bowl and serve very hot.

✳ Mushrooms and Bean Curd Soup

✳ TUNG SUN TOU FU T'ANG

10 dried mushrooms
6 cups chicken stock
3 squares bean curd
1½ teaspoons salt

Wash the mushrooms and soak in 1 cup warm water for about 10 minutes. Steam them and cut them in half. Put in a saucepan with the chicken stock and mushroom liquid. Bring to a boil and simmer for about 6 minutes. Cut the bean curds into ½-inch cubes and add to the soup with the salt. Simmer for another 5 to 7 minutes and then serve very hot in a deep bowl.

✳ Pork with Red Bean Curd Cheese

✳ NAN JU JO

1 pound pork, cut into
   1-inch cubes
2 teaspoons oil
1 clove garlic, crushed
½ teaspoon salt
1 teaspoon soy sauce

1 tablespoon sherry
1 teaspoon sugar
2 tablespoons bean curd cheese
   in sauce (nan yu)
2 cups soup stock

Heat a pan with the oil, garlic and salt and stir once or twice. When the oil is very hot add the pork and sauté for 2 minutes. Add the soy sauce, sherry and sugar and continue to stir for 1 minute. Add the bean curd cheese and stir thoroughly. Slowly pour the soup into the pan and when it comes to a boil, lower the heat, cover and simmer for 20 minutes or until the pork is tender. Serve in a bowl.

NOODLES

✳ Ch'ao Mien Foochow Style

✳ FU CHOU CH'AO MIEN

2 tablespoons oil for pork
½ pound pork, shredded
3 stalks scallions, cut into
   1-inch sections
5 mushrooms, soaked and
   sliced

½ pound medium broad noodles
generous amount of water
3 tablespoons oil for noodles
2 tablespoons beef stock
1 tablespoon sherry

Heat a pan with oil and sauté pork, scallions and mushrooms for about 10 minutes, stirring constantly. Transfer to a plate and set aside.

Boil the noodles in a generous amount of water for about 10 minutes, or until they are barely tender. Pour into a colander,

184

rinse with cold water and set aside to drain well. Heat the pan again with 3 tablespoons oil and add the noodles. Brown them well for about 12 minutes, stirring constantly, and then slowly add ¾ of the pork mixture, and continue to cook for another 2 or 3 minutes. Add the beef stock to moisten the mixture and stir once or twice again. Turn the noodles onto a large hot platter and garnish with the remainder of the pork mixture, and sprinkle with sherry. Serve very hot.

✳ Vegetarian Noodles

✳ CH'ING TS'AI CH'AO MIEN

1 *bamboo shoot*	*Thickening:*
1 *cup washed spinach*	1 *teaspoon cornstarch*
8 *mushrooms, soaked*	*mixed with*
2 *tablespoons pickled cabbage*	2 *teaspoons soy sauce*
¼ *pound medium broad egg noodles*	*mushroom water*
generous amount of water	2 *tablespoons sherry*
1 *tablespoon oil*	*pepper and salt to taste*

Slice the bamboo shoot into shreds 1½ inches long. Wash the spinach and drain well. Soak the mushrooms in 1 cup of boiling water for 30 minutes and then slice. Wash the pickled cabbage and slice. Boil the egg noodles in a generous amount of water for 10 minutes, rinse in a colander and drain well.

Heat a pan with oil, add the bamboo shoot and sauté for 2 minutes. Add the spinach, mushrooms and pickled cabbage and continue to cook for 3 minutes, stirring constantly. Add the egg noodles, mix well with vegetable and cook for 2 minutes. Add thickening to the noodles and bring to a boil. When the sauce becomes smooth and thick, add the sherry, correct the seasoning with salt and pepper, and serve at once.

✳ Pan-Fried Noodles with Chicken Livers

✳ CHI KAN CH'AO MIEN

½ pound thin noodles	Thickening:
2 tablespoons oil	2 tablespoons cornstarch
1 pound chicken livers	mixed with
¼ cup chopped celery	4 tablespoons water
¼ cup chopped onions	2 teaspoons soy sauce

Boil the noodles in a generous amount of water for 10 minutes. Turn into a colander, rinse in cold water and set aside to drain. When well drained, chill thoroughly in a refrigerator.

Heat a 7-inch skillet with oil; when it is very hot, add half the noodles, and brown on both sides. Transfer onto a hot serving platter and keep warm. Repeat with the remainder of the noodles.

Cut the chicken livers into small pieces and put into the oily skillet with celery and onions. Sauté over moderate heat (adding a little more oil if necessary), stirring constantly, for 5 minutes. Add thickening to the chicken livers, stirring constantly, until the sauce is smooth and thick. Correct the seasoning, pour over noodles and serve very hot.

✳ Noodles with Lobster and Vegetables

✳ LUNG HSIA CH'AO MIEN

½ pound medium broad noodles	Thickening:
enough oil to fry noodles	1 teaspoon cornstarch
¼ pound cooked lobster meat	mixed with
¼ pound fresh mushrooms	½ tablespoon water
1 onion, finely sliced	¼ teaspoon sesame seed oil
1 bamboo shoot, finely sliced	dash of white pepper
½ teaspoon salt	
⅛ teaspoon pepper	

Boil the noodles in a generous amount of water for 10 minutes, turn into a colander and rinse with cold water. Drain well.

Heat 1 inch of oil in a deep 8-inch skillet. Add the noodles and press them firmly against the sides and bottom of the pan. Cook for a few minutes till the noodle cake holds its shape, but before it turns brown. Remove the cake to a hot serving plate and keep it warm.

Drain away the surplus fat from the skillet, but leave the pan oily. To it, add the lobster meat, mushrooms, onion and bamboo shoot, and sauté for 1 minute. Season with salt and pepper and continue to stir for 1 minute more. Add thickening to the mixture and cook till the sauce is smooth and clear. Pour it over the noodles and serve very hot.

✳ Noodles with Chicken, Ham and Oysters

✳ CHI JO HUO T'UI LI LUANG MIEN

¼ pound medium broad egg
    noodles
enough water for boiling noodles
2 ounces Smithfield ham
4 cups chicken stock
1 cup oysters
¼ teaspoon salt
1 slice ginger, chopped fine
2 stalks scallions, finely chopped

1 tablespoon oil for chicken
¼ pound chicken, thinly sliced
6 mushrooms, soaked and sliced
2 stalks leeks, quartered and
    thinly sliced
4 pieces tree fungus, soaked
2 tablespoons soy sauce
2 tablespoons sherry

Boil the noodles in a generous amount of water for about 10 minutes. Turn into a colander, rinse in cold water and drain well.

Cut the Smithfield ham into shreds 1½ inches long and simmer in the chicken stock for 5 minutes. Add the oysters, salt and ginger and continue to simmer for another 10 minutes. Add the noodles and the scallions and when it becomes hot, cook for another 2 minutes. Set aside the pan and keep it warm. Just before serving, divide the noodles into individual bowls and keep warm.

Heat a pan with the oil and sauté the chicken and mushrooms. Add the leeks, wood ear and soy sauce and sauté for 5 minutes, stirring well. Sprinkle with sherry, arrange over noodles in individual bowls and serve very hot.

✳ Noodles in Thick Gravy

✳ LU MIEN

½ pound medium broad egg
    noodles
generous amount of boiling water
5 mushrooms, soaked
10 dried shrimps, soaked
4 pieces tree fungus, soaked
1 tablespoon oil
½ pound pork, sliced thin
2 stalks scallions, cut into
    1-inch lengths
2 eggs, well beaten
salt and pepper to taste

1 tablespoon soy sauce
½ tablespoon sherry
¼ cup seasoned water
4 cups chicken stock

Thickening:
4 tablespoons cornstarch
mixed with
6 tablespoons seasoned water

Bring a large saucepan of water to a boil, add the noodles and let cook for 15 minutes. Pour into a colander, rinse with cold water and set aside to drain. Put into a double boiler to keep hot, and just before serving transfer to a large heated bowl.

Soak the mushrooms, shrimps and wood ear for ½ hour in hot water; drain them, reserving the seasoned water. Slice the mushrooms.

Heat a pan with oil and sauté the pork for 2 minutes. Add the mushrooms, wood ear and scallions and cook together for another 3 minutes. Season with soy sauce, sherry and ¼ cup seasoned water; add half the chicken stock and the shrimps. Bring to a boil, add the rest of the chicken stock gradually, lower the heat and simmer for 20 minutes. Add thickening to the liquid and bring to a boil. It should be as thick as heavy cream; if it is not, add a little more thickening paste. Pour the eggs slowly into this *Lu* mixture, stirring constantly. Correct the seasoning with salt and pepper. Pour over the noodles in a large bowl and serve immediately.

✳ Soy Paste Noodles

✳ CHA CHIANG MIEN

½ *pound medium broad noodles*
generous amount of water
  2 *tablespoons oil*
  ¾ *pound minced pork*
  1 *slice ginger, chopped fine*
  2 *stalks scallions, finely chopped*
  1 *clove garlic, crushed*
  6 *tablespoons vegetable*
      paste (Hoisin)

½ *cup water*

Accompaniments:
½ *cucumber*
10 *radishes*
  3 *stalks celery*
  5 *stalks scallions*

Boil the noodles in a generous amount of water for 10 minutes. Turn into a colander, rinse with cold water and set aside to drain.

Arrange in small dishes the following raw vegetables: finely chopped scallions, the cucumber and radishes cut into shreds, the celery into thick shreds and blanched in salted boiling water. Refrigerate all of these.

Heat a pan with oil and sauté the pork in it, adding ginger, scallions and the garlic. Stir for 4 or 5 minutes, separating the particles of meat in the process. Add the soy bean paste and continue to cook till the paste is very hot. Add water, stirring constantly, and cook for 10 minutes longer. Pour into serving bowl and place on the table with the other cold vegetables.

Serve the noodles in individual bowls and let each guest help himself to the meat mixture and vegetables which should be mixed thoroughly with the noodles.

✳ Chicken Lo Mien

✳ CHI JO LO MIEN

½ pound fine egg noodles
generous amount of water
 2 tablespoons oil
 1 cup cooked chicken, shredded
 1 cup sliced celery cabbage
 1 cup sliced celery
 1 cup bean sprouts
 1 teaspoon sugar
 1 cup chicken stock

Thickening:
1½ tablespoons cornstarch
mixed with
 2 tablespoons water
 2 tablespoons soy sauce

salt and pepper to taste
 2 stalks scallions, chopped fine

Boil the egg noodles in a generous amount of water for 10 minutes.
Turn into a colander, rinse in cold water and set aside to drain.

Heat a pan with the oil, add the chicken and toss for 2 minutes.
Add the cabbage, celery, bean sprouts and sugar and stir for 1
minute. Add the chicken stock, stir well and cover the pan; turn
down the heat and simmer for 10 minutes. Add thickening and
stir constantly till the sauce is smooth and thick. Correct the
seasoning with salt and pepper to taste. Add the noodles, stir
gently and when mixture is very hot, turn onto a deep platter,
sprinkle with the scallions and serve immediately.

✳ Rice Noodles with Vegetables

✳ CHING TS'AI MEI FEN

½ pound rice noodles
 2 tablespoons oil
½ cup shredded pork
½ cup shredded bamboo shoots
 1 cup celery cabbage

2 cups chicken stock

Thickening:
 2 teaspoons cornstarch
 4 tablespoons water

Boil the noodles in a generous amount of water for 10 minutes. Turn into a colander, rinse in cold water and set aside to drain. Heat pan with oil, brown the noodles lightly, and when they are very hot, transfer to a warm serving platter.

Add to the oily pan the pork, bamboo shoots and cabbage and sauté for 2 minutes. Add the chicken stock, cover, turn down the heat and cook for another 5 minutes. Add the thickening to the sauce and cook till it becomes smooth and thick. Pour over the fried noodles and serve very hot.

✳ Vermicelli with Sherry and Eggs

✳ CHIU TAN KUA MIEN

½ pound vermicelli
8 cups water
3 cups chicken stock
2 tablespoons sherry
3 tablespoons soy sauce

1 tablespoon oil
2 stalks scallions cut into 1-inch
   lengths
3 eggs

Bring 8 cups of water in a saucepan to a boil, add the vermicelli and boil for 20 minutes. Pour into a strainer, rinse in cold water and set aside to drain. Put in a double boiler to keep warm.

Heat the stock, add sherry and soy sauce and keep warm. Divide the vermicelli into individual bowls and keep warm. Heat a pan with the oil, add the scallions and sauté for 1 minute. Add the eggs and scramble them, stirring constantly. While the egg mixture is still liquid, add the stock mixture and stir well. When it comes to a boil and before it is completely coagulated, pour over the bowls of vermicelli and serve at once.

RICE

There are different types of rice, many varieties within the types, and many grades within a variety; but generally speaking there are two main types, the ordinary rice and the glutinous rice. The rice we encounter every day is also divided into two—the long-grained and the oval. The Chinese, as a general rule, prefer the long-grained variety while the Japanese favor the oval. The oval type rice takes longer to cook and less water to produce the same consistency as the long-grained rice. The amount of water needed to cook rice varies with personal preference, depending on how hard or soft you like your rice. If you like your rice soft, add a little more water when boiling. But according to the Chinese, all rice, to be edible, should be dry with all moisture absorbed by the rice. One cup of raw rice makes about 2 cups of cooked rice.

In a Chinese meal rice occupies the same place as bread or potatoes in a Western meal; it is the staff of life in China.

Glutinous rice, or sweet rice as it is often known in this country, is used by the Chinese for dumplings, puddings and other special dishes which call for sticky rice. A little of this rice may also be added to congee to make it thicker and stickier. Unless glutinous rice is specified, ordinary rice is to be used in the following recipes.

✳ Boiled Rice

✳ FAN

2 cups rice   3½ cups water

Wash the rice in two changes of water. Cover the rice with water, making allowance for amount of water remaining on rice when measuring, and bring to a boil. Lower heat, cover, and simmer 20 to 30 minutes or until completely fluffy. Serve at once.

✳ Steamed Rice

✳ CHEN FAN

1 cup rice   2 cups water

Wash the rice in two changes of water, add water and bring to a boil; boil for 3 minutes. Turn this rice into individual bowls, only half filling them to allow for expansion.

Put a rack in a large saucepan filled to 1½ inches of boiling water. Place the bowls on the rack, making sure that the boiling water won't overflow into the rice, and steam for about 1½ hours. Steamed rice will be of looser texture than boiled rice.

✳ Congee—Soft Rice

✳ HSI FAN

¾ cup long-grained rice   8 cups water
¼ cup sweet or glutinous rice

Wash the rice in two changes of water and then add the 8 cups water. Bring to a boil, turn down the heat, cover and simmer for about 2 hours, stirring once or twice every 20 minutes, when it should be thick and smooth.

Serve with salted nuts, scrambled eggs, bean curd cheese, *jo sung* and pickled vegetables, or anything which will spice up the bland rice.

✳ Crisp Rice

✳ CHA FAN

The left-over crispy, crusty rice at the bottom of the pan and the left-over glutinous rice may be made into appetizers and crisp chips to serve with drinks.

Break the crusty rice into pieces the size of potato chips. The glutinous rice, being sticky, may be formed into desired shapes. Heat a deep frying pan with oil and when it is very hot lower a few pieces of rice into it and fry till they are golden brown. Remove and drain well. Sprinkle with pepper and salt. Serve either hot or cold.

✳ Fried Rice with Beef and Peppers

✳ CH'ING CHIAO CH'AO FAN

1 *pound filet steak*

Marinade:
  1 *tablespoon soy sauce*
  mixed with
  ½ *teaspoon sugar*
  2 *tablespoons cornstarch*
  2 *tablespoons sherry*

4 *tablespoons oil*
2 *onions*
1 *green pepper, shredded*
4 *cups cold, cooked rice*
2 *teaspoons soy sauce*
¼ *teaspoon white pepper*

Cut the meat against the grain into shreds 1½x¼ inch. Mix with the marinating mixture and let it stand for 10 minutes.

Heat a pan with 2 tablespoons oil and when it is very hot add the meat and sauté for 2 minutes. Remove and set it aside. Sauté the onions till they become brown, add the green pepper and stir 1 minute or till it turns bright green. Remove the vegetables and set them aside. To the same pan add the remaining oil and when it is hot add the rice and sauté for 2 minutes, making sure that the grains are well separated. Add the onions, green pepper and beef, and mix well together. Sprinkle with soy sauce and white pepper. Turn off the heat, stir again once or twice and then serve in a shallow bowl immediately.

✳ Fried Rice with Chicken

✳ CHI TING CH'AO FAN

2 eggs, well beaten	4 tablespoons cooked chicken, diced
4 tablespoons oil	
½ teaspoon salt	½ cup peas
4 cups cold, cooked rice	1 bamboo shoot, diced
½ onion, diced	½ Chinese sausage, diced
2 tablespoons ham, diced	2 teaspoons soy sauce
4 mushrooms, soaked and diced	2 tablespoons cooked shrimps, diced

Make an omelet with the eggs, and cut it into strips 1 inch long and ¼ inch wide. Set these aside.

Heat a pan with 2 tablespoons oil and ½ teaspoon salt. When it is very hot add the rice and sauté for 5 minutes. Remove and set aside. Add the remaining 2 tablespoons oil to the hot pan and brown the onion. Add the rest of the ingredients and sauté for 3 minutes. Slowly add the rice and when it is well mixed, stir in the soy sauce and the shredded eggs and when it is very hot, turn off the heat. Stir once or twice and turn into a shallow bowl and serve at once.

✳ Fried Rice with Oyster Sauce

✳ HAO YU CH'AO FAN

1 *pound roast pork, diced*	2 *tablespoons oyster sauce*
3 *tablespoons oil*	4 *eggs*
3 *cups cooked, cold rice*	

Heat a pan with oil and sauté the pork for 1 minute. Add the rice and stir well, separating the grains with chopsticks or spatula, for about 3 minutes. When the rice is well coated with oil, add the oyster sauce and continue to stir for 1 minute more. Break the eggs one by one and stir into the rice; when they start to coagulate, turn into a shallow bowl and serve immediately.

✳ Eggs and Rice

✳ CHI TAN CH'AO FAN

3 *eggs, well beaten*	4 *cups cold, cooked rice*
4 *tablespoons sherry*	4 *tablespoons shredded ham*
½ *teaspoon salt*	½ *cup chicken stock*
3 *tablespoons oil*	2 *slices bamboo shoots,*
	shredded fine

Beat the eggs well, add sherry and salt and set aside. Heat a pan with oil, slowly pour in the eggs and stir rapidly; the moment it begins to thicken add the dry rice and keep stirring. Add the chicken stock and half of the ham and stir constantly until the rice is very hot. Remove from the fire and turn into a large serving bowl. Garnish with the remaining shredded ham and bamboo shoots. Serve immediately.

* Fried Rice with Beef

5 cups cooked, cold rice
3 tablespoons oil for rice
¼ pound filet beef
1 tablespoon soy sauce

1 tablespoon oil
2 onions, shredded
½ pound celery cabbage,
   shredded
½ teaspoon salt

Heat a pan with oil and when it is very hot stir in the rice. Sauté for about 4 minutes, taking care to separate the grains.

Cut the beef into 1½-inch shreds, mix with the soy sauce, and let stand for a few minutes. Heat a smaller pan with 1 tablespoon of oil, and when it is hot sauté the onion until transparent, stirring constantly; add the cabbage and sauté, continuing to stir. Finally add the meat and sauté for 1 minute. Remove this pan from the heat and reheat the rice. Combine the meat with the rice and mix well together. When it is very hot, turn onto a shallow platter and serve very hot.

* Fried Rice with Shrimps

4 mushrooms, soaked and diced
4 tablespoons shrimps
2 stalks scallions, cut into 1-inch
   sections
2 slices bamboo shoots, diced
2 tablespoons diced ham

½ teaspoon salt
5 cups cooked, cold rice
3 small eggs, well beaten
1 teaspoon soy sauce
1 tablespoon oil
3 tablespoons oil for rice

Wash and soak the mushrooms in ½ cup hot water for 30 minutes and then stem and dice. Shell and devein the shrimps and dice into the same size. Heat a pan with oil and when it is hot sauté the mushrooms and bamboo shoots for 1 minute. Add the shrimps, ham, scallions and salt. Stir once or twice and then set aside.

Heat a large pan with the 3 tablespoons oil and when it is very hot add the rice and stir vigorously. Separate the rice with chopsticks or spatula and when it is very hot, add all other ingredients except eggs and mix well. Pour the eggs in last, raise the heat for 30 seconds and then turn it off. Keep stirring till the eggs coagulate. Turn into a shallow bowl and serve immediately.

DESSERTS

✳ Eight Precious Pudding

✳ PA PAO FAN

1½ cups glutinous rice
3½ cups water
½   cup sugar
12 dates or dragon's eyes
24 raisins
12 candied lotus seeds

12 almonds, blanched

Sauce:
½   cup sugar
1   tablespoon cornstarch
1   cup boiled water

Boil the glutinous rice in 3 cups of water for about 15 minutes
or until soft. Add the sugar and another ½ cup water and simmer for 15 minutes more. Rub the bottom of a pudding bowl
with a little oil and arrange the fruit and nuts in a pleasing pattern. Spoon the rice into the bowl without disturbing the fruit
and fill the bowl ¾ full. Place in a steamer and steam for 3 hours.

Boil the sauce mixture together for 5 minutes and have it boiling just before serving the pudding. Turn the pudding out onto a flat dish and pour the hot sauce over it. Serve very hot. Any fruit or nuts may be substituted for the lotus seeds and dragon's eyes if these are not available. When making substitutions, keep in mind the color contrast on the white rice.

❋ Peking Dust

❋ LI-TZU NI

1 *pound chestnuts*	2 *tablespoons confectioners*
pinch of salt	*sugar*
	2 *cups whipped cream*

Boil the chestnuts for 40 minutes or until well cooked. Shell and blanch them and pass through a sieve. Add salt and sugar and mix well. Put through a ricer and shape into a mound on a serving platter. Cover the chestnuts with a thick topping of whipped cream and serve cold.

❋ Candied Bananas

❋ HSIANG CHIAO TANG

4 *firm bananas*	3 *tablespoons cornstarch*
2 *tablespoons oil*	½ *teaspoon finely chopped*
1 *teaspoon white sugar*	*ginger*
⅔ *cup vinegar*	½ *teaspoon salt*
⅔ *cup brown sugar*	1 *large bowl ice water*

Peel the bananas and cut them in half lengthwise. Heat a pan with the oil and white sugar. Sauté the bananas over low heat till they start to turn brown. Set aside in the pan.

Place the vinegar, brown sugar, cornstarch, ginger and salt in a saucepan and bring to a slow boil over medium heat, stirring constantly. Boil for about 2 minutes, and then pour the liquid over the bananas in the skillet; continue to cook over low heat for about 2 minutes. Place in a serving bowl after plunging each piece of banana into ice water for about 30 seconds to harden the candy coating. Serve immediately.

✳ Steamed Pears

✳ CHEN LI

4 medium-sized cooking pears	2 teaspoons powdered cinnamon
8 teaspoons honey	

Cut off about 1 inch from the top of the pears. Scoop out the core from the center without making a hole right through the fruit. Fill the holes with honey and cinnamon, cover with the tops of the pears and place in ovenproof individual dishes in which they will be served. Steam from half an hour to an hour, depending on the size and ripeness of the fruit, until the fruit is cooked through. Serve very hot.

✳ Almond Junket

✳ HSING JEN KAO

1 cup evaporated milk	1 envelope gelatin
3 tablespoons sugar	3 tablespoons water
3 cups water	3 teaspoons almond extract

Heat milk, sugar and water till the sugar is melted and the liquid very hot but not boiling. Mix the gelatin in 3 tablespoons water and add slowly to the hot liquid. Stir till the gelatin is completely dissolved. Set aside and cool and then add the almond extract and mix well. Pour into a cake pan and refrigerate. In 3 or 4 hours or when it has gelled, cut into small cubes. Half fill an almond bowl (a bowl smaller than a rice bowl) with this junket and cover with cold sweetened water. Serve chilled.

✳ Date Cakes

✳ TSAO NI PING

2 cups pitted dates	½ cup blanched walnuts, chopped fine
1 cup water	
1 tablespoon lard	⅓ cup sugar
1 cup glutinous rice flour	1 tablespoon sesame seeds
	drop of oil

Wash the dates, bring to a boil in 1 cup of water and simmer for about 20 minutes or till the water is all evaporated. Skin the dates and pass through a sieve. Add the lard and the glutinous flour and knead well. Roll out into a long roll about 1 inch in diameter and cut into ½-inch pieces. Flatten these pieces out thin.

Sauté the sesame seeds in a little oil for about 2 seconds, add the walnuts and sugar and toss for another 2 seconds. Put a teaspoon of this mixture on each piece of dough and shape into a ball. Roll balls lightly in flour and place on a square of waxed paper, seam side down. Steam for 15 minutes and serve very hot. Will make about 20 small cookies.

✳ Green Pea Cake

✳ CHING TOU PING

½ pound split green peas	2 tablespoons cornstarch
½ cup sugar	4 tablespoons water
2¼ cups water	

Soak the peas for about 1 hour and then bring to a boil and simmer for 1½ hours. Put the purée through a fine sieve and return to the saucepan. Add the sugar and the cornstarch, mixed with a little water, and bring to a boil again, stirring constantly. Turn the heat low and simmer for 1 minute. Pour into a shallow tray and cool in the refrigerator. When set, cut into 1-inch cubes and serve.

✳ Almond Cookies

✳ HSING JEN PING

1½ cups flour	pinch of salt
½ teaspoon baking powder	¾ cup sugar
½ cup sesame seed oil	1 egg
¼ cup ground almonds	20 whole blanched almonds
½ teaspoon almond extract	

Sift the flour and baking powder in a mixing bowl. Slowly add the oil and mix well. Add the almonds, almond extract, sugar, salt and whole egg and stir thoroughly. This should be a stiff dough, but if it is too stiff to work with, add a drop of water at a time till the dough is pliable. Form into small balls and press into cookies ½ inch thick and about 2½ inches in diameter. Place an almond in the center of each cookie. Place on lightly greased cookie sheet and bake in a preheated oven at 350 degrees for about 15 minutes or until they are light brown in color. Cool and serve.

✳ Fortune Cookies

3 eggs	½ cup flour
½ cup confectioners sugar	½ teaspoon lemon extract

Beat eggs with an electric beater for 2 minutes. Add sugar gradually, beating for 10 minutes. Fold in flour and lemon extract and continue to beat for another 2 minutes.

Turn an electric grill to medium heat, drop a tablespoonful of batter till it spreads to about 3 inches in diameter. Cook ½ minute on each side or till cakes become golden brown. While they are still hot and pliable, place a fortune-telling paper in center, and fold up the cake from 3 sides. Allow to cool. Will make about 30 cookies.

✳ Almond Tea

✳ HSING JEN CH'A

8 level tablespoons almond paste   3 cups cold water

Mix the almond paste with water in a blender turned on to fine. Put the liquid, when blended, through a sieve of 6 layers of cheesecloth. Heat in a double boiler till very hot, but just under the boil. Serve very hot in small almond bowls.

✳ Orange Tea

✳ CHÜ-TZU T'ANG

3 medium oranges
½ cup glutinous flour
enough water to form a stiff
    dough

½ cup sugar
5 cups water

Cut the oranges in half, scoop out the pulp and juice and set all aside in bowls. Add a teaspoon of water at a time to the flour till it forms a stiff dough. Roll dough into small balls the size of marbles and set them aside. Bring the sugar and water to a

boil and drop the flour balls into this liquid. Continue to boil
till they float. Add the orange and the juice to the liquid, bring
to a boil and cook for another 10 seconds. Serve very hot in small
almond bowls.

✳ Plum Sauce

✳ HSING LI CHIANG

1 cup plums	½ cup vinegar
1 cup apricots	1 cup sugar
½ cup apple sauce	½ cup chopped pimiento

Remove the skins and stones from the plums and apricots. Mix
all the ingredients together and bring to a boil. Lower the heat
and simmer for about 1 hour. Pour into airtight jars while liquid
is still hot and keep in a cool, dark place for 1 month. To serve,
add a little water and sugar to taste.

✳ Soy Bean Jam

✳ CHIANG YU CHIANG

2 cups soy beans	1 tablespoon salt
1½ tablespoons sugar	6 cups boiling water

Mix all ingredients together and place in a saucepan. Bring to a
boil, turn down the heat and simmer for 3 hours or till the water
is all evaporated. Stir occasionally during the process. Pour into
airtight jars and place in a cool, dark place for 6 months.

PASTRY

✳ Steamed Bread

✳ MAN T'OU

½ envelope yeast
2 tablespoons sugar
¼ teaspoon salt

1 scant cup warm water
2 cups flour

Dissolve the yeast in water with the sugar and salt. Add flour to the liquid and knead into a soft dough for about 10 minutes. Put in a large bowl, cover with a damp cloth and place in a warm place for about 1 hour to rise to double its size. Knead again and let rise to double its size once more. Roll and stretch the dough into a rope about 1½ inches in diameter. Cut into 1-inch sections and roll into ovals about 4 inches long. Make them a bit thinner in the center, dust the whole side with a little flour and double over. Put on squares of wax paper for 15 or 20 minutes or till they double in bulk. Put in a steamer for 10 to 15 minutes to steam. They should be light and spongy. Serve hot with "red-cooked" dishes.

✳ Steamed Dumplings

✳ PAO-TZU

Filling:
  1 pound celery cabbage
  ½ pound ground pork
  1 stalk scallion, finely chopped
  1 tablespoon soy sauce
  ½ teaspoon sugar
  1 teaspoon salt
  ½ tablespoon sesame seed oil

Dough:
  ½ envelope yeast
  1 cup lukewarm water
  2½ cups flour
  a little extra flour for dusting

Chop the cabbage very fine, put in a towel and squeeze out the liquid. Mix the cabbage with the rest of the filling ingredients and put in a refrigerator for about 4 hours to congeal.

Dissolve the yeast in warm water and add the flour. Knead dough on a floured board until it is dry. Place in a large basin, cover with a damp cloth and let it rise till it quadruples in bulk (in about 4 hours). Punch the dough down and knead it again, using a little dusting flour to keep the dough from sticking to the fingers. Roll the dough into a long cylinder and divide into 10 parts. Roll these pieces into rounds about 3 inches in diameter. Hold the dough in the palm of the left hand and put 2 tablespoons of filling in the center. With the thumb and index finger of the right hand turn the rim of the circle to cover the stuffing and pinch the edges together, until only a small opening is left in the center. Place a piece of wax paper on the side opposite the hole. Place in a steamer, well separated to allow for expansion, and steam from 20 to 30 minutes. Serve very hot.

✳ Sautéed Dumplings

✳ KUO T'IEH

½ pound celery cabbage
1 teaspoon salt
½ teaspoon sugar
¾ pound pork
½ teaspoon salt for pork
2 teaspoons sugar
1½ tablespoons sherry
1 teaspoon soy sauce
¼ pound shrimps

½ teaspoon sesame seed oil
¼ cup water

Wrapping mixture:
2 cups sifted flour
½ cup warm water
1 tablespoon oil
½ cup water

Dice the cabbage fine and sprinkle with 1 teaspoon salt and ½ teaspoon sugar. Let it stand for 15 minutes or till the water is drawn out of the cabbage. Cut the pork and chop fine with a cleaver. This workout is important as it makes the meat juicy. Put in a large bowl, add the salt, sugar and sherry and mix well. Be sure to add the sherry first and then the soy sauce, as this is the secret of a tasty filling. Shell and devein the shrimps and cut up fine. Add the cabbage and ¼ cup water to the meat mixture; then add the shrimps. If the mixture is too dry, add a little water. When the mixture is at the consistency desired, add the oil. If you want the filling juicy, make the mixture early and put it in the refrigerator to congeal; it will be easier to handle.

Wrapping: Put 1½ cups of sifted flour in a large bowl and slowly add the warm water, using chopsticks. Do not use your fingers as too much handling will harden the dough. If it is too sticky use the remaining flour to stiffen it. Start to knead before the flour is properly worked into the dough. Stretch and roll the dough to a rope about 1 inch in diameter. Cut pieces about 1 inch thick and roll into rounds 4 inches in diameter, making the edges thinner than the center because the edges will be doubled. Place a heaping teaspoon of meat into the center and pinch into shape.

Heat 1 tablespoon oil in a heavy skillet. Arrange the dumplings in a circle around the perimeter of the pan, each facing the same way. Fill the center with the dumplings in a pleasing pattern. Cover and cook over medium heat until the bottoms turn golden brown and begin to crackle. Add ½ cup water, cover the pan and continue to cook until the water has all evaporated. Loosen the dumplings from the pan with a spatula and invert them on a plate.

Serve with side dishes of chopped ginger, vinegar and soy sauce.

✳ Spring Rolls

✳ CH'UN CHÜAN

Filling:
  ½ pound pea sprouts
  ¼ pound shrimps
  ½ pound pork
  6 stalks scallions
  3 tablespoons oil
1½ teaspoons sugar
  ½ teaspoon salt

Wrapping:
  2 cups flour
  1 cup water
  a little oil

enough oil for deep frying

Make a soft dough with flour and water and knead well. Dust the board to prevent sticking. Stretch the dough into a rope 1 inch in diameter and cut into 20 equal pieces. Roll into flat rounds about 5½ inches in diameter. Moisten them lightly with oil and cook pancakes in a hot pan without oil till they are lightly brown.

Wash the pea sprouts and pick them over. Shell and devein the shrimps and dice them. Dice the pork fine and cut the scallions into 1-inch lengths.

Heat a pan with oil and when hot, sauté the pork and the shrimps for 1 minute. Add the scallions and the pea sprouts and stir for another 2 minutes. Add the sugar and salt and stir once or twice. Remove from the heat. Place 2 heaping teaspoons of the filling on the baked side of each wrapping and fold it into a long package like a roll. Wet the ends with water and close securely.

Heat pan and fill up to 1 inch of oil. Deep-fry the rolls for 6 minutes or until they turn golden brown. Serve very hot with soy sauce.

✳ Cantonese Egg Rolls

✳ CHI TAN CHÜAN

Wrapping:
2 eggs
½ cup water
½ teaspoon salt
¾ cup flour
1 teaspoon oil

Filling:
1 stalk celery
1 stalk scallion
½ cup shredded pork, cooked
½ cup chopped raw shrimps
1 teaspoon salt
2 teaspoons sugar
⅛ teaspoon pepper

Oil for frying

Beat the eggs and put aside a teaspoon of it for sealing purposes. Mix remaining eggs with water and salt, then add the flour to make a thin batter. Heat a pan with oil and pour in enough batter to make a thin pancake about 5 inches in diameter, rolling the pan to make the batter spread evenly. Cook for about 1 minute, then peel pancake off the pan and place on a damp towel. Continue till you have used up all the batter.

Shred the celery and blanch for 3 minutes. Set it aside to drain. Chop the scallion fine and combine with the pork, shrimps, salt, sugar and pepper. Add the celery and mix well. Put a heaping tablespoon of filling on the cooked side of each wrapping, fold edges and roll up. Seal with the beaten egg and set the rolls aside for about 1 hour. Heat a pan with 1 inch of oil and when it is boiling hot, fry the rolls for about 5 minutes or until brown, turning frequently. Serve hot with side dishes of soy sauce.

✳ Pork and Water Chestnut Dumplings

✳ SHAO MAI

Wrapping:
- 1 egg, well beaten
- ½ cup water
- 1½ cups sifted flour

Filling:
- 1 cup chopped pork
- 4 water chestnuts
- 1 bamboo shoot
- 1 teaspoon cornstarch
- ¼ teaspoon salt
- ¼ teaspoon sugar
- dash of white pepper

Make a dough with the egg, water and flour. Knead well until smooth and elastic. Cover with a wet cloth and let stand for 10 minutes. Roll out the dough as thin as possible and cut into 2½-inch squares and wrap in a damp cloth.

Mince the chopped pork, peeled water chestnuts and bamboo shoot separately. Add the cornstarch to the meat and mix well. Add the water chestnuts, bamboo shoot, salt, sugar and pepper. Put a heaping teaspoon of filling in the center of each wrapping and bring edges up and pinch together. There should be a wide opening at the top to show the filling. Put on a flat plate over rack and steam for 30 minutes. Serve hot with side dishes of soy sauce.

✳ Stuffed Balls

✳ T'ANG T'UAN

Dough:
- ½ pound glutinous rice flour
- ½ cup warm water

Filling:
- ½ pound ground pork
- 2 tablespoons soy sauce
- ½ teaspoon sugar
- 1 teaspoon sherry
- 1 stalk scallion, chopped fine
- 1 tablespoon cornstarch
- ½ teaspoon sesame seed oil

Mix the ingredients for the filling well together, and set aside in the refrigerator to congeal.

Mix the warm water with the rice flour and knead for about 5 minutes. Stretch into a long rope and cut into 24 pieces. Make each piece of dough into a ball and then make an indentation big enough to put a teaspoon of filling in. Pinch the dough over the filling and roll into a ball again.

Boil 6 cups of water in a saucepan and lower the balls into the water. When water boils again, cook the balls for 5 minutes or until they start to float. Add 1 cup of cold water to the saucepan to harden the balls. Bring the water to a boil again and cook for another 2 or 3 minutes. Serve in individual bowls with the liquid.

✳ Onion Cakes

✳ TS'UNG YU PING

1 bunch scallions	1½ cups flour
1 teaspoon salt	½ cup water
sesame seed oil	2 tablespoons oil

Wash the scallions well, chop fine, sprinkle with salt and set aside. Mix the flour and water together to form a soft dough. Stretch into a long rope about 1½ inches in diameter. Cut into 1-inch lengths and roll these into small pancakes about ⅛-inch thick. Pour a few drops of sesame seed oil on the pancakes and sprinkle with the chopped scallions. Roll up tightly, and then press the ends together between the palms of the hands till pancakes are about ¼ inch thick. Give each roll a twist, one palm going clockwise and the other counterclockwise. You can then see the swirls and the green scallions. Pan-fry for a few minutes on each side. Serve hot as a savory

✳ Meat Dumplings

✳ CHIAO-TZU

Filling:
  1 pound lean pork
  6 stalks scallions
  1 slice ginger, chopped fine
  1 teaspoon soy sauce
  1 pound celery cabbage
  2 tablespoons sesame seed oil
  6 leeks (white part only),
    finely chopped
  1 teaspoon salt

Wrapping:
  2 cups sifted flour
  ½ cup cold water

Put the pork and scallions through a food chopper and add the ginger and soy sauce. Mix well. Chop the cabbage fine, put in a towel, and squeeze to extract as much water as possible. Mix the cabbage thoroughly with the meat mixture and add the sesame seed oil. Finally add the leeks and season with salt. Place in the refrigerator.

Mix the flour with water to form a soft dough. Stretch and roll dough in a rope about 1 inch in diameter. Cut pieces about 1 inch long and roll into rounds about 4 inches in diameter. Place about 1½ teaspoons filling in each round of dough, fold over, pinching the edges together with thumb and index finger to seal.

Bring a large saucepan of water to boiling point, drop in the dumplings and boil for about 8 minutes or until they are cooked through. Serve 4 or 5 in individual bowls with side dishes of soy sauce, vinegar and pepper.

The above quantities will make about 20 medium-sized *chiao tzus*.

PART*III

SUGGESTED MENUS

✳ Menus for Two

I

Lobster Cantonese
Sweet and Sour Spare Ribs
White Rice
Fresh Fruit

II

Minced Pork with String Beans
Broiled Squab
White Rice
Candied Bananas

III

Diced Chicken with Almonds
Steamed Fish with Mushrooms
White Rice
Almond Cookies

IV

Sautéed Shrimps with Peas
Chicken Sautéed with Hot Pepper
White Rice
Steamed Pears

217

V

Shredded Pork with Pea Sprouts
Deep-Fried Chicken
White Rice
Orange Tea

VI

Egg Pockets
Braised Chicken with Sweet
  Peppers
White Rice
Almond Junket

✳ Menus for Four

I

Abalone Soup
Minced Beef with Salted Cabbage
Sautéed Broccoli
Paper-Wrapped Chicken
Eggs Foo Yong
White Rice
Fresh Fruit

II

Chinese Mustard Greens Soup
Sweet and Sour Chicken Livers
Bean Sprouts and Pork
Barbecued Beef
Steamed Sole in Savory Custard
White Rice
Almond Cookies

III

Ham and Cabbage Soup
Bean Curd with Sea Bass
Fried Pork Balls
Beef with String Beans
Diced Chicken with Almonds
White Rice
Almond Tea

IV

Cream of Crab Soup
Beef with Green Peppers
Steamed Eggs with Minced Pork
Savory Squabs
Bean Sprouts and Celery
White Rice
Canned Lichees

V

Beef and Turnip Soup
Steamed Sea Bass
Celery with Mushrooms
Broiled Squabs
Boiled White Chicken
White Rice
Green Pea Cake

VI

Egg Drop Soup
Paper-Wrapped Chicken
Steamed Pork with Salted
  Cabbage
Phoenix-Tail Shrimps
Creamed Chinese Cabbage
White Rice
Candied Bananas

✳ Menus for Six

I

Watercress Soup
Roast Pork
Pike Sautéed with Chinese Vegetables
Savory Egg Custard
Red-Cooked Chicken with Chestnuts
Beef with Mushrooms
White Rice
Fresh Fruit

II

Lotus Stem Soup
Barbecued Spare Ribs
Fried Shrimps
Braised Chicken with Mushrooms
Beef with Green Peppers
Carp Sautéed with Ginger
White Rice
Candied Bananas

III

Ham and Cabbage Soup
Tea Eggs
Red-Cooked Duck
Beef with String Beans
Shrimp Balls
Cauliflower, Water Chestnuts and Mushrooms
White Rice
Almond Tea

IV

Mushrooms and Bean Curd Soup
Deep-Fried Chicken Livers
Red-Cooked Flounder
Beef with String Beans
Steamed Eggs with Minced Pork
Sautéed Chinese Broccoli
White Rice
Green Pea Cake

V

Chinese Mustard Greens Soup
Cantonese Sausage
Chicken Velvet
Szechuan Duck
Beef with Cauliflower and Snow Peas
Steamed Eggs with Shrimps
White Rice
Canned Lichees

VI

Fresh and Salt Pork Soup with Bamboo Shoots
Stuffed Mushrooms
Bean Curd with Sea Bass
Steamed Pork with Ground Rice
La-tzu Chi—Peppered Chicken
Cucumber Salad
White Rice
Steamed Pears

❋ Menus for Ten

I

HORS D'OEUVRES

Ham
Chicken Gizzards
Tea Eggs
Roast Pork

SMALL DISHES

Sautéed Shrimps with Peas
Fried Quail
Minced Pork with String Beans
Beef Sautéed with Snow Peas

LARGE DISHES

Winter Melon Soup
Steamed Pork with Ground Rice
Red-Cooked Chicken with
    Chestnuts
Peking Duck
Sweet and Sour Carp
Fried Noodles

DESSERT

Eight Precious Pudding
Orange Tea

II

HORS D'OEUVRES

Chicken Livers
Cantonese Sausage
Preserved Eggs
Celery

SMALL DISHES

Shrimp Balls
Savory Squabs
Beef with Green Peppers
Paper-Wrapped Chicken

LARGE DISHES

Chinese Mustard Greens Soup
Braised Pheasant
Red-Cooked Pork Shoulder
Szechuan Duck
Bean Curd with Flounder
Fried Rice

DESSERT

Peking Dust
Almond Tea

❋ Buffets for Twelve

I

Chungking Watermelon Soup
Peking Duck
Steamed Bread
Eight Precious Pudding

II

Szechuan Duck
Red-Cooked Shin of Beef
Curried Lamb

Sweet and Sour Carp
Vegetable Chop Suey
White Rice
Almond Tea

III

Winter Melon Soup
Red-Cooked Pork Shoulder
Turkey à la Chinoise
Sweet and Sour Carp
Creamed Chinese Cabbage

Fried Rice with Shrimps
Peking Dust

IV

West Lake Steamed Duck
Curried Chicken

Carp Sautéed with Ginger
Barbecued Spare Ribs
Cucumber Salad
Ch'ao Mien Foochow Style
White Rice
Almond Junket

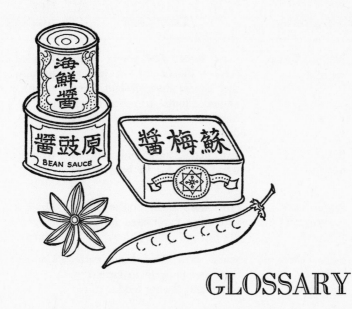

GLOSSARY

The ingredients listed below are all available at Oriental food stores (Chinese and Japanese) throughout the country. When available elsewhere, as in supermarkets, they are so marked. Most of the ingredients are imported, but some are locally grown and canned. In the first column the names are given in English and in the *Kuo yu* Romanization. The phonetic version of the names in Cantonese is given in the second column in order to facilitate their purchase. In smaller grocery stores where English is not spoken, either show them the Chinese characters or ask for the ingredients in the Cantonese dialect.

❋ Ingredients	Description	How Available
Abalone PAO YÜ	BAO YÜ A large mollusk. Prolonged cooking renders it rubbery, therefore cook as little as possible.	Dried by weight or canned.

* Ingredients	Description	How Available
Bamboo Shoots TSU SUN	JOOK SOON The young ivory-colored shoots are cut just as they appear above ground. Keep unused shoots in water in refrigerator and change water daily.	Canned. May be found in some supermarkets.
Beans, Black HEI TOU	HAK DAO Wash and soak in warm water for ½ hour before using.	By weight.
Beans, Black, Fermented TOU SHIH	DOW SEE Small crushed bean with spicy flavor used for cooking fish and other dishes.	Dried by weight or canned.
Bean, Yellow Paste TOU CHIANG	WONG DOW Soy bean paste. Salty and pungent in taste. Preserves and flavors food.	Canned.
Bean Curd TO FU	DOW FOO The precipitated protein matter of soy beans. Junket-like.	By pints, singly in squares, or canned.
Bean Curd Cheese TOU FU JU	FOO YU Fermented bean curd. Shaped in 1-inch squares. Tastes like Camembert.	In jars.
Bean Curd Cheese in Sauce NAN JU	NAN YU Fermented bean curd prepared in brick-red sauce.	Canned.
Beans, Red TOU SHA	HUNG DOW For making sweet black bean fillings.	By weight.
Bean Sprouts TOU YA	DA DOW NGAH Specially grown soy bean sprouts, gold in color. Coarser than pea sprouts.	Fresh by weight or canned. In supermarkets.

* Ingredients	Description	How Available
Bird's Nest YEN WO	YEN WO A certain kind of swallow catches fish during the summer and keeps most of it in the nest to feed the young in winter. The bird also digests a certain kind of marine plant which is transformed into a gelatinous matter with which it makes its nest. It has been found that the nests contain vitamins and other nourishment and swallows' nests are considered one of the most nutritious and delicious of foods.	Shredded and dried.
Broccoli, Chinese KAI LAN TS'AI	GUY LAN CHOY Very popular Chinese vegetable.	By weight.
Cabbage, Chinese PAI TS'AI	BAK CHOY Vegetable with green leaves and white stems.	By weight.
Cabbage, Celery SHANTUNG PAI TS'AI	Long white stalks resembling a head of celery in shape but more tightly packed.	By weight. In supermarkets.
Cabbage, Fermented P'AO TS'AI	MUY CHOY Pickled cabbage.	By weight.
Cabbage, Salted HSIEN TS'AI	HARM CHOY Dried. Wash and soak in cold water for ½ hour.	By weight.
Chestnuts, Water PI CHI	MAH TUY Root of marsh plant, used as a vegetable. Must be peeled.	Fresh by weight. Peeled in cans.
Dried Foods	To prepare most Chinese dried foods for cooking, rinse and soak them for about 30 minutes in a little warm water. Liquid may be used for cooking.	Usually by weight.

* Ingredients	Description	How Available
Dates, Chinese Red HUNG TSAO	HOONG JOE Jujubes. Small with leathery-looking skins. Used in soups, fish dishes and desserts.	By weight.
Dragon's Eyes LUNG YEN	LOONG GUARN Resembles ly-chees with smooth cinnamon-colored shells.	Dried in boxes, by weight and canned.
Eggs, Preserved P'I TAN	PEI DAN Peel off the black lime and the shell and wash. The white of the egg is gelatinous, the yolk cheeselike.	Singly.
Egg Roll Wrapping CH'UN CHÜAN PI	CHAN GIN PEI Wrapping made of egg dough cut into squares. Should be kept in a wet towel in refrigerator.	By weight.
Egg, Salted HSIEN TAN	HARM DAN Must be boiled. Whites will be very salty and yolks bright orange.	Singly.
Fish, Dried HSIEN YÜ	HARM YU Very salty.	By weight.
Five Spices WU HSIANG	A ready-mixed combination of Chinese star anise, fennel, Chinese anise pepper, clove and Chinese cinnamon.	By weight.
	Star anise: PA CHIAO BAAK GOR (*Illicium anisatum*) Star-shaped seed with 8 points. Used for red-cooking.	
	Fennel: HUI HSIANG TOU WOO HEUNG (*Foeniculum vulgare*) Pale green seeds.	
	Chinese anise pepper: HUA CHIAO	

* Ingredients	Description	How Available
	FAH JIU (*Xanthoxlum piperitum*) Reddish seed. Used for cooking fish.	
	Clove: TING HSIANG DING HEUNG (*Jambosa caryophyllus*) Dark brown cloves.	
	Chinese cinnamon: JO KUEI YOOK GWEY (*Cinnamomum cassia*) Similar to stick cinnamon, but more powerful aroma.	
Fungus, Tree MU ERH	WEN YEE A dried black fungus also known as wood or cloud ear.	By weight.
Ginger Root CHIANG	SANG GEURNG Tuber with hot spicy flavor. Looks like gnarled fingers. Sometimes used unpeeled.	Fresh by weight.
Ginkgo Nuts PAI KUO	PAAK KWO Crack nuts and soak nut meat in hot water and blanch.	By weight. Canned.
Lotus Seeds LIEN TZU	LIEN JEE Seeds of lotus flower. Available candied during Chinese New Year.	By weight.
Lotus Stems LIEN O	LIEN NGOW Red-brown starchy tuberous stems of the lotus. Used as a vegetable.	Dried by weight. Canned.
Melon, Bitter KU KUA	FOO GWAH Also known as Balsam Pear. A vegetable the size of a cucumber, green and wrinkled. Presence of quinine gives the bitter taste. Layer of white spongy pulp inside must be discarded.	Fresh by weight.

* Ingredients	Description	How Available
Melon Seeds KUA TZU	KWA JEE Dried like nuts.	By weight.
Melon, Winter TUNG KUA	DOONG GWA A large melon used as a vegetable.	Fresh by weight.
Monosodium Glutamate WEI CHING	MEI CHING There are many commercial makes of this gourmet powder. Brings out food flavors.	In jars or cans.
Mushrooms, Chinese TUNG KU	DOONG KOO Dried, brownish-black, capped mushrooms. Soak in warm water ½ hour before using. Fresh mushrooms may be substituted.	By weight.
Mustard Greens, Chinese KAI TS'AI	KAI CHOY Green leafy vegetable with many nodes and a bitter taste.	By weight.
Needles, Golden CHIN CHEN	GUM CHOY Dried lily flowers. Cut in 2-inch lengths. Used in fish, poultry and vegetable dishes.	By weight.
Noodles, Egg CHI TAN MIEN	DAN MIEN Made with eggs.	Fresh. Dried. In super-markets.
Noodles, Pea Starch FEN SSU	FEN SEE Crisp, dry, transparent vermicelli.	Dried in boxes.
Noodles, Rice MI FEN	MEI FEN MIEN Small, thin, easily broken, not transparent.	Packaged.
Oysters, Chinese Dried HAO KAN	HO SEE Red-brown in color. To flavor soups and stews.	By weight.
Oyster Sauce HAO YU	HO YOW Extract of cooked oysters. Used as a flavoring.	In bottles or canned.

* Ingredients	Description	How Available
Parsley, Chinese YUAN SUI	YIN SAY (Coriander) Has flat serrated leaves of medium-green color. Highly aromatic. Should be used sparingly.	In bunches.
Pea Sprouts TOU YA	NGAH CHOY Tiny white pea shoots with olive-green hoods. Delicate.	Fresh by weight or canned. In supermarkets.
Peas, Snow HSÜEH TOU	HSI DOW *or* HAW LAHN DOW Tender pea pods with no parchment lining. Picked before peas form and eaten whole. Also known as *mange tout*.	Fresh by weight.
Pickled Vegetable CHA TS'AI	CHA CHOY A form of pressed, pickled cabbage.	Canned.
Rice, Glutinous NO MI	NOR MEI A variety of rice which becomes very sticky when cooked.	By weight.
Rice, Sweet NO MI	Same as above.	By weight and packaged.
Pepper-and-Salt Mix CHIAO YEN	Heat ⅔ pepper and ⅓ salt in a skillet for 5 minutes. Cool and store in shaker. Table condiment for fried foods.	
Sausage, Cantonese LA CH'ANG	LUP CHONG A red-and-white pork sausage. Looks waxy when cold.	By weight.
Scallops, Dried KAN PEI	GON YAU JEE Gold-colored, very flavorful. Used in soups and other dishes.	By weight.
Seaweed, Dried TZU TS'AI	CHEE CHOY In purplish sheets. Used in soups. Contains iodine.	By weight or packaged.

* Ingredients	Description	How Available
Sesame Paste CHIH MA CHIANG	JEE MA CHERNG Difficult to find. Peanut butter is a good substitute.	Canned.
Sesame Seed Oil CHIH MA YU	JEE MA YAU Fragrant, aromatic salad oil. Used to flavor soups and other dishes.	In bottles.
Shrimps, Dried HSAI MI	HAR MEI Tiny and hard. Soak in hot water for about 15 minutes. Used as flavoring.	By weight.
Shrimp Sauce HSIA YU	HAR MA CHEUNG A salty flavoring used in Fukien cooking.	In jars or canned.
Soy Jam CHU YU	A thick sweet and salty soy paste. Residue of soy sauce.	Canned.
Soy Bean Skin FU TSU	FOO JOOK Creamy-colored, dried bean curd skin.	By weight.
Soy Sauce, Light CHIANG YU	JEUNG YOW Locally made, used for cooking.	In jars and bottles.
Soy Sauce, Thick CHIANG YU	JEUNG YOW Imported and suited for table condiment or for special cooking.	In bottles.
Squash, Chinese MU KUA	FAHN GWAH A variety of marrow, larger than a cucumber, with yellow stripes.	Fresh by weight.
Vegetable Paste HAI HSIEN CHIANG	HOI SIN Salty, red seasoning sauce used in cooking shellfish and duck.	Canned.
Wan Tun Skins YUN T'UN P'I	Wrappings made of egg and flour. Square in shape.	Fresh by weight.

CHINESE
FOOD MARKETS

In many of the large cities in the United States there is at least one Chinese grocery store which carries ingredients mentioned in this book. Those marked with an asterisk are willing to fill mail orders.

✳ California

Farmer's Market—Chinese
  Kitchen
West 3rd and Fairfax
Los Angeles, California

Yee Sing Chong Company*
960 Castelar Street
Los Angeles 12, California

Kwong on Teong
720 Webster Street
Oakland, California

Wing Chong
367 8th Street
Oakland, California

Fung Chong Company
1001 Grant Avenue
San Francisco, California

Mow Lee Sing Kee Company*
730 Grant Avenue
San Francisco, California

✳ Illinois

China Farms
733 West Randolph Street
Chicago 6, Illinois

Min Sun Trading Company*
2222-2228 South La Salle Street
Chicago 16, Illinois

✳ Massachusetts

See Sun Company*
36 Harrison Avenue
Boston, Massachusetts

Tung Hing Lung Company
9 Hudson Street
Boston, Massachusetts

✳ New York

Eastern Trading Company*
2801 Broadway
New York 25, New York

Wing Fat Company*
33-35 Mott Street
New York 13, New York
Attention: Mr. James Lai

✳ Pennsylvania

Wing On Grocery Store
1005 Race Street
Philadelphia, Pennsylvania

✳ Texas

Cheng Mee Company*
712 Franklin Street
Houston, Texas

Taiwan Company
811 Chartres Street
Houston, Texas

✳ Washington, D. C.

Mee Wah Lung Company*
608 H Street, N.W.
Washington, D. C.

New China Supply Company
709 H Street, N.W.
Washington, D. C.

INDEX

Bean curd (cont'd)
  with mushrooms, 181
  with scallions, 180
  with sea bass, 177
  with shrimps, 180
Bean sprouts
  beef with, 173
  celery and, 174
  pork and, 174
Beans
  mung, used to grow bean
    sprouts, 172
  string
    beef with, 129
    lamb with, 136
    minced beef with, 130
    minced pork with, 118
  See also Soy beans
Beef, 120-132
  and peppers, fried rice with,
    194
  and small Chinese cabbage in
    oyster sauce, 125
  and turnip soup, 52
  balls, minced, with spinach,
    131
  barbecued, 123
  braised, 122
  fire pot, 146
  five flavor, 120
  kidney, sautéed, 139
  meat balls, sweet and sour, 132
  minced
    with beans, 130
    with salted cabbage, 130
  sautéed with asparagus, 123
  sautéed with celery cabbage,
    125
  sautéed with snow peas, 128
  shin of, red-cooked, 121
  spiced, 121
  with bean sprouts, 173
  with cauliflower and snow peas,
    124
  with green peppers, 126
  with mushrooms, 127

Beef (cont'd)
  with onions, 127
  with radishes, 128
  with string beans, 129
Birds, see Chicken, Duck; Pheas-
    ant; Quail, Snipe; Squab
Boiling, 15
Bread, steamed, 206
Broccoli, Chinese, sautéed, 163

❋ C ❋

Cabbage
  braised, with mushrooms, 164
  celery,
    beef sautéed with, 125
    filling for dumplings, 207,
      209
    with chestnuts, 166
  Chinese
    creamed, 165
    small, beef and, in oyster
      sauce, 125
  salted
    minced beef with, 130
    steamed pork with, 113
Cabbage and ham soup, 53
Cabbage hearts, Chinese, with
    crab-meat sauce, 164
Cake, green pea, 202
Cakes
  date, 202
  onion, 212
Cantonese school of cooking, 9
Carp
  sautéed with ginger, 57
  sweet and sour, 58
Cauliflower
  beef with snow peas and, 124
  water chestnuts and mush-
    rooms, 166
Celery
  as an hors d'oeuvre, 46
  bean sprouts and, 174
  with mushrooms, 167